# THE FAITHFUL OF CHRIST

The New Canon Law for the Laity

# THE FAITHFUL OF CHRIST

English Paraphrase of the New Canon Law
Applicable to
the Laity with Select Commentary

by John M. Huels, O.S.M., J.C.D.

FRANCISCAN HERALD PRESS
1434 WEST 51st STREET • CHICAGO, 60609

*The Faithful of Christ, English Paraphrase of the New Canon Law Applicable to the Laity with Select Commentary* by John M. Huels, O.S.M., J.C.D. Copyright © 1983 by Franciscan Herald Press.

**Library of Congress Cataloging in Publication Data**

Huels, John M.
   The faithful of Christ.

   Includes index.
   1. Canon law.   I. Catholic Church. Codex Juris
Canonici.   II. Title.
LAW        262.9′4         83-20531
ISBN 0-8199-0873-8

Nihil Obstat:
   Rev. James O'Connor
   *Censor Librorum*

Imprimi Potest:
   Very Rev. Augustine M. Kulbis, O.S.M.

Imprimatur:
   Joseph Cardinal Bernardin
   Archbishop of Chicago

November 21, 1983

MADE IN THE UNITED STATES OF AMERICA

*For my Mother*

# TABLE OF CONTENTS

# Preface

"The faithful of Christ" is the term used by the 1983 Code of Canon Law for a member of the Church—*christifidelis* in Latin. This term includes all members of the Church whether cleric, religious, or lay, and so the use of the term as a title indicates that this book is meant for all Catholics. Its purpose is modest but important: to make the Church's laws more accessible to all its members, especially the laity. It has often been said that the laity were "rediscovered" by the Church at the Second Vatican Council. The Council recognized their unique role and special contributions to the Church's life and ministry, and the revised Code of Canon Law reflects this awareness with its many canons on the faithful in general and on the laity in particular.

I have selected canons or paragraphs of canons from all seven books of the Code which are applicable or may be of interest to the faithful in general or to the lay faithful in particular. Where necessary or desirable, I have commented briefly on certain canons or sections of the Code to explain their meanings or provide additional information. The Introduction explores the nature and role of law in the Church.

The potential uses for this book are several. Among these it can serve as a reference of church laws for laypersons; as a supplementary text for a high school or adult religious education class; as an introduction to canon law; or it can be read simply to satisfy the curiosity of those Catholics who want to know how the Code applies to them. It might also stimulate the reader to explore specific topics further in a detailed canonical commentary or in the Code itself.

The English paraphrase of the canons aims for accuracy of meaning without a slavish adherence to the grammatical structure and wording of the original. In keeping with the non-specialist nature of my audience, I have avoided a literal translation of technical terms which may not be understood or may even be confused by the person not versed in canon law. For example, instead of translating *christifidelis* as the "Christian faithful" which could be understood as including all Christians, I use the terms "the faithful" in the plural or "a member of the faithful" in the singular. Instead of translating *sacri ministri* as "sacred ministers" which sounds almost blasphemous in English, I have rendered it "ordained ministers;" *sacri pastores*—"sacred pastors"—is paraphrased "church authorities" to distinguish this more general term from that for pastors of parishes—*parochi*. Since a grammatically exact and technically precise translation is not intended, one should refer to the Latin original for complete authenticity and authority.

*J. H.*
*November 27, 1983*

# INTRODUCTION
# THE NATURE AND ROLE OF CANON LAW

On January 25, 1983 Pope John Paul II promulgated a revised Code of Canon Law which took effect on the first Sunday of Advent of that year. This was a historic date because on January 25, 1959—24 years earlier—Pope John XXIII had first announced the project to revise the Code while at the same time he called for an ecumenical council, the famous Vatican II. Since the Council we Catholics have seen many changes in our Church's life, liturgy, and discipline. Most of these changes in Church law were enacted during the 15-year pontificate of Paul VI. By and large these laws are incorporated in the revised Code, but there are some new laws in it as well. Before looking at some of the actual contents of this revised Code, it would be useful to ask some more fundamental questions: What is canon law? How does it differ from other Church disciplines? Why do we need law in the Church? What is its purpose and role?

## What Is Canon Law?

The term "canon" comes from the Greek word for a rule or a straight rod, and from this meaning it also came to refer to any kind of norm or normative rule. A canon, then, is a rule or a short statement of the law. The Code is an organized collection of laws in canon form. The first Code of Canon Law was promulgated in 1917. The purpose of this first codification was to make the Church's laws available to more people by reducing their number and putting them in one small book. Before 1917 it was often very difficult even for the experts to know what all the laws were because they were compiled in massive collections. These collections contained laws which originated from popes, councils, and other sources over a span of many centuries. The 1917 Code adopted only those laws which were still relevant, added some new ones, and abrogated most of the old ones, leaving a relatively small law book of 2414 canons. This made it much easier for people to know the law and to apply it. The revised Code of 1983 is somewhat shorter with 1752 canons.

To better understand what canon law is, we should be clear on what it is not. First, canon law is not doctrine. Church doctrine includes the authoritative teachings of the magisterium on issues of faith, such as the doctrine of the Holy Trinity, the doctrine of the divine and human natures of Christ, or the doctrine of the Immaculate Conception. One would seldom find such beliefs in the Code, although the Code does contain some doctrinal canons such as c. 749 on the infallibility of the pope and the ecumenical council. However, the insertion of such doctrinal canons in the Code is generally intended to lay the theological groundwork for the *disciplinary* canons which are based on them. The overall nature of the Code therefore is disciplinary, not doctrinal. The disciplinary canons are genuine ecclesiastical, or Church, laws. Some examples of disciplinary laws include the regulations on fast and abstinence; the precept of Mass attendance and rest on Sundays and holy days; the law of the Easter duty; regulations for the reception of the sacraments, such as requirements of age and preparation. Other ecclesiastical laws of the Code establish structures and norms regulating numerous aspects of the Church's visible life at all levels, from the pope to the person in the pew.

While canon law is not doctrine, it is also distinct from ethics or morals. When some people hear of the law of the Church they think of the Ten Commandments, or of teachings on moral issues such as abortion and euthanasia. These latter are not mere ecclesiastical laws but are considered to be derived from the divine law. Divine law is revealed in scripture or tradition, or we know it by our human reason—the so-called natural law. For example, the sin of murder is part of the divine natural law. It is not merely church law because human reason tells us that it is wrong to kill other persons. We also know that murder is wrong because of the Fifth Commandment which, coming from scripture, makes it part of the divine positive law. Divine laws bind everybody, not just Catholics. Church law, however, applies only to Roman Catholics with few exceptions. An example of a purely ecclesiastical law is the precept of Sunday Mass attendance. It is based on the divine law (thou shalt keep holy the Lord's day), but the way this divine law is enfleshed—the precept to attend Mass on Sunday—puts it in the realm of ecclesiastical law binding only Catholics.

Let's take another example. Several times I have heard people ask the question: Why are priests allowed to be laicized and to get married, yet the Church will not allow lay people to get divorced and remarried? The answer lies in the difference between divine law and merely ecclesiastical law. The law of celibacy requiring priests to remain unmarried is merely a disciplinary law of the Church. For many centuries of Christian history priests were allowed to marry, and a pope or an ecumenical council could some day let them marry once again. Church law is changeable. By contrast, divine law cannot be changed by the Church because divine law comes from God. The Church understands the teaching of Jesus on divorce as divine law: "What God has joined together, let no one put asunder" (Mk 10:9). The Church believes it does not have the power to change its position on divorce and remarriage because the words of Christ in the gospel have already settled the issue.

The divine law, whether it comes from scripture, from the natural law, or from doctrine, cannot change. Often there are fuller understandings of the divine law by later generations as a result of new insights, but the basic kernel of truth behind the divine law is eternal. Laws of the Church, on the other hand, can change and do change. Changes in Church law, as in civil law, are necessary to keep pace with changes in human society and culture. Changing circumstances in the history of the Church and the world require changes in the Church's discipline. Many of us have witnessed vast changes in Church law in our own lifetimes following Vatican II. These changes, as important as some of them were, do not touch the essentials of the faith but deal only with the external aspects.

## What Is the Purpose of Canon Law?

This may seem like a very basic question, but we have to examine it because there are some people who say the Church does not need law. "We have the freedom of the children of God," they claim. "We have the Holy Spirit to guide us; we have our bibles; we don't need anything else. Besides, law is oppressive—all rules and regulations. Christ came to set us free from the law. Can't we just follow our consciences without the hierarchy telling us what to do?" In light of such attitudes we must ask: why canon law?

The purpose of canon law in the Church is the same as that of law in any society. Whenever human beings get together and form groups or associations of whatever kind, they inevitably make laws. In pre-civilized, illiterate societies, there is always some customary law, a law of the tribe. A family has its own rules, as does a school or business. When an organization is founded some constitutions or by-laws are drawn up. Even when children build a clubhouse they make certain rules: "Only members allowed;" "no entry without the password;" "anyone who reveals the password is out of the club"—a true excommunication!

Just as all human groups have law, so too does the Church because the Church is fully human. To deny this is tantamount to denying the Incarnation itself. In Christ, God became a human being, died and rose from the dead, and founded a Church of disciples, the holy people of God who are at the same time real people with all their weaknesses. Truly God sent the Holy Spirit as a divine guide and inspiration for the Church, but that does not take away the Church's humanity. As in all human groups, so also in the Church there must be law. Laws preserve peace, harmony, and unity in the community. Laws are intended to promote the common good and also to protect personal rights. Without law, there would be no freedom because the opposite of freedom is not law but chaos, and without law we would truly have chaos and anarchy.

Laws establish structures and procedures which usually operate without our even being conscious of them. A good example of this is a charismatic prayer meeting. When I first went to such a meeting some years ago I was astounded by what seemed to be the complete spontaneity of the meeting. It all ran very smoothly and beautifully, seemingly a movement entirely of the Holy Spirit without human organization. But after attending a few times I began to notice repeated patterns and I soon recognized that there was a definite structure to the meetings which provided the framework for the freedom of the Spirit. This structure was the result of conscious planning and effort by the group's leadership. The most successful charismatic prayer groups are those which are well planned and well run, and which have a team of able, prayerful leaders. The groups which think that reliance on the Holy Spirit excuses them from planning and organization are the groups that flounder and die. We seldom notice the structures and organization—the legal system—which lies behind a group's visible functioning, but we would certainly notice the bad effects on the group if that legal system was deficient.

Since laws in Church and society are so necessary, why do people complain about law and structure? Why do some politicians campaign successfully against "big government"? Why do people try to get around the law? The problem is not with the concept of law itself, but rather with particular laws which restrict us from doing something we want to do, or which make us do something we don't want to do. Nobody likes to pay taxes. Many do not like driving at only 55 mph. However, these restrictions on our freedom as individuals are intended to serve the good of society as a whole.

In any system of law, there is always a built-in tension between the good of the community and that of the individual. What is this tension? Law very often places limits and checks on individual freedoms, rights, and charisms as well as provides mechanisms to protect them. If there were no limits on individuals they could do entirely as they please—steal, perjure, murder, etc.—and this would lead to chaos. On the other hand, laws can sometimes go too far in the other direction and take away basic individual freedoms. For example, communist societies frequently are too protective of the common good, and individual liberties suffer as a result. By contrast, the legal system of the United States has tended too often to favor the rights of individuals even to the detriment of society—the rights of criminals who can be freed on a technicality; the rights of the rich who use loopholes in the law and pay no taxes; the rights of gun owners to have private arsenals. American gun laws are among the most liberal in the civilized world, but the citizens of this country are also the victims of more murders than any other comparable nation. Good law looks for a happy balance between the rights of the individual and the good of society.

Church law too can become imbalanced. Before Vatican II the Church was overly centralized and hierarchical at the expense of the individual charisms and talents of all its members. Even lay members of the Church often developed a legalistic mindset, looking to the law to provide answers to nearly every question of life and religion. In the years following Vatican II there was too often an over-reaction to this legalistic past. "We don't need any law in the Church," some said. "As long as we believe in God and are good people, we can conduct our own affairs. We don't need all those rules and regulations of the Church." Such attitudes were not uncommon.

What is needed is not the abolition of law, but the creation of good law, a law that balances individual rights with the good of the community. The answer is neither unnecessary restrictions on individual freedoms nor a rejection of all law and authority, but a law which can reduce the tension between freedom and authority, between the individual and the group. When law fails to accomplish this, the cooperation of men and women of good will is needed to work for constructive change. Such harmonious cooperation is especially needed in the Church because it is not only a human society but also is the Spirit-filled body of Christ.

The making of the 1983 Code involved such cooperation. There were widespread consultations and numerous revisions in the period from the announcement of the project to pro-mulgation. The result is a law book which is much more up-to-date than the 1917 Code and far more useful to a wide spec-trum of the universal Church. However, as great an improve-ment as the revised Code may be, it does not mean the end of change and reform in the Church. The Church is not the king-dom but is on the way to the kingdom, and therefore it must always be about the task of reforming itself. The on-going task of reform in the Church requires on the part of all the virtues of charity, patience, and humility, and continued dedication de-spite the fact that the Church may seem to some to be moving too slowly or too quickly. The task of reform also requires men and women of faith and hope who are confident that the Holy Spirit is with the Church at all times. Trusting in the Spirit as our invisible, divine guide, we can more readily accept the law of the Church as a visible and earthly guide—human and im-perfect as the Church itself—but an important help to us as we journey to the kingdom.

# Book I
# General Norms

The first book of the Code has 203 canons covering various general principles of canon law. For the most part these are rather dry, technical norms which are not of great interest to the ordinary Catholic. The canons which follow were selected because they are of greater relevance and interest to a general audience.

*Latin Rite Code*

> Canon 1. The canons of this Code pertain only to the Latin rite.

The Catholic Church has many different rites, such as the Ukrainians, Ruthenians, Maronites, Melkites, etc., but the largest rite by far is the Latin rite. The Eastern Churches have their own code of law.

## Subjects of the Law

> Canon 11. Those bound to observe merely eccle-
> siastical law are those baptized into the Catholic
> Church or received into it, who enjoy a sufficient use
> of reason and, unless the law expressly states other-
> wise, have reached the age of seven.

Cc. (canons) 11–13 distinguish those who are bound to observe the laws of the Church, and those who are not. The basic
principle is that Catholics who have the use of reason and are
at least seven years old are subject to the law.

## Universal and Particular Laws

> Canon 12,1. Everyone for whom a universal law has
> been enacted is bound to observe that law
> everywhere.
> 2. However, when a universal law is not in force in a
> certain territory, all who are in that territory are
> exempt from observing it.
> 3. In the case of laws enacted for a particular terri-
> tory, they bind only those who have a domicile or
> quasi-domicile and are actually staying there, with
> the exception of the cases mentioned in c. 13.

All Catholics are bound to observe *universal* laws which apply to them such as the law of the Sunday Mass obligation.
Universal laws of the Church bind everywhere except where
there may be contrary customs or privileges or particular ex-
emptions from the law. For example, canon law prescribes ten
holy days of obligation, but in the United States and other
countries some of these are not observed as days of precept and
others are transferred to Sundays. Unlike universal laws
which bind everywhere, *particular* laws of a certain territory,

such as a diocese, are in force only for those who live in that territory, with some exceptions mentioned in c. 13.

## Personal Laws

> Canon 13,1. Particular laws are not presumed to be personal but rather territorial, unless otherwise evident.

Personal laws bind persons wherever they go. For example, a religious sister is bound by her constitutions wherever she goes. Laws are not presumed to be personal unless it is clear that they are. Instead, laws are presumed to bind only in the territory for which they are made.

## Travellers

> Canon 13,2,n.1. Travellers are not bound by particular laws of their own territory as long as they are absent from it, unless the transgression of such a law would cause harm in their own territory, or unless the laws are personal.
> 2. Travellers are not bound to the laws of a territory in which they are travelling, except for those which pertain to public order, determine the solemnity of acts, or pertain to immovable things located in the territory.

Since particular laws bind as a rule only the residents of the territory, travellers are not generally bound to observe particular laws, except as noted above.

## Wanderers

> Canon 13,3. Wanderers (*vagi*) are bound to both universal and particular laws in the place where they are staying.

Unlike travellers, wanderers are persons who have no place of residence—no domicile or quasi-domicile. They are bound to both universal laws and the particular laws of whatever diocese or territory they are in at the time.

## Physical Persons

> Canon 96. By baptism one is incorporated into the Church of Christ and becomes a person in the Church with the duties and rights proper to Christians according to their condition to the extent that they are in ecclesiastical communion and are not impeded by a sanction legitimately imposed.

All baptized Christians are members of the Church, but only those who are Catholic are bound to the duties of Church law. Some basic duties and rights of all the faithful and of the lay faithful are given in cc. 208–231. The baptized who are in full communion with the Catholic Church are defined in c. 205. Sanctions are treated in Book VI of the Code.

## Adults, Minors, Infants

> Canon 97,1. One who is 18 years old or older is a major person; below this age, a minor.
> 2. A minor under the age of seven is called an infant and is considered incompetent (*non sui compos*); at the age of seven, one is presumed to have the use of reason.
> Canon 98,1. Major persons have the full exercise of their rights.
> 2. Minor persons remain subject to their parents or guardians in the exercise of their rights, with the exception of those areas in which minors are exempt from parental control either by divine law or by canon law. In reference to the designation of guardians

and their functions, the civil law should be observed unless canon law establishes something else, or if, in certain cases and for a just cause, the diocesan bishop has decided to provide for the appointment of another guardian.
Canon 99. Whoever habitually lacks the use of reason is considered incompetent and is classified as an infant.

The age of majority in canon law is 18, and the attainment of this age has legal consequences. For example, an 18-year old is bound to fast on Ash Wednesday and Good Friday. The age of seven is also important in canon law because this is the age at which the law presumes the use of reason has been attained, and legal consequences follow from that presumption. For example, one who is seven and has the use of reason may, in accord with the law, receive all the sacraments except holy orders and marriage.

## Distinction of Persons as to Place

Canon 100. A person is called a *resident* when in the place of one's domicile; a *temporary resident* when in the place of quasi-domicile; a *traveller* if going outside one's domicile or quasi-domicile while still retaining it; a *wanderer* if one does not have a domicile or quasi-domicile anywhere.

## Place of Origin

Canon 101,1. The place of origin of a child, including a convert, is that in which the parents had a domicile or quasi-domicile when the child was born or, if the parents did not have the same domicile or quasi-domicile, that of the mother.
2. If it is a question of a child of wanderers, the place

of origin is the place of birth itself; if the child was abandoned, it is the place where the child was found.

## Domicile and Quasi-Domicile

Canon 102,1. Domicile in the territory of some parish or at least of a diocese is acquired by residence there together with the intention to remain there perpetually, if nothing calls one away; or by having lived there for five years.

2. Quasi-domicile in the territory of some parish or at least of a diocese is acquired by residence there together with either the intention of remaining there for at least three months, if nothing calls one away, or by actually living there for three months.

3. Domicile or quasi-domicile in the territory of a parish is called parochial; in the territory of a diocese, even if not in a parish, it is called diocesan.

## Domicile of Spouses

Canon 104. Spouses have a common domicile or quasi-domicile; by reason of legitimate separation or for some other just cause, both may have their own domicile or quasi-domicile.

## Domicile of Minors

Canon 105,1. Minors necessarily retain the domicile or quasi-domicile of those who have authority over them. Those who are beyond infancy are able to acquire their own quasi-domicile; and those who have been legitimately emancipated according to the norm of civil law may acquire their own domicile.

2. Whoever has been placed legitimately in the tu-

telage or care of another for some reason other than minority has the domicile or quasi-domicile of the tutor or guardian.

## Loss of Domicile or Quasi-Domicile

Canon 106. Domicile or quasi-domicile is lost by departure from a place with the intention of not returning, without prejudice to c. 105.

## Proper Pastor and Ordinary

Canon 107,1. One's pastor and ordinary are those of the place of domicile or quasi-domicile.
2. The proper pastor or ordinary of a wanderer is the pastor or ordinary of the place in which the wanderer is actually staying.
3. The proper pastor of those who have only a diocesan domicile or quasi-domicile is the pastor of the place in which they are actually staying.

## Consanguinity and Affinity

Canon 108,1. Consanguinity is computed by lines and degrees.
2. In the direct line there are as many degrees as there are generations, that is, as there are persons, not counting the common ancestor.
3. In the collateral line there are as many degrees as there are persons in both lines, not counting the common ancestor.
Canon 109,1. Affinity arises from a valid marriage, even if not consummated, and it exists between a man and the blood relations of his wife and also between a woman and the blood relations of her husband.

2. It is computed such that those who are blood rela-
tives of the man are related by affinity to his wife in
the same line and degree as they are related by consanguinity to the man, and vice versa.

The determination of one's line and degree of consanguinity
or affinity in relation to another is at times necessary to see if
one meets an eligibility requirement, such as a couple who
wish to marry but are related to each other either by blood or
by the marriage of another family member. Consanguinity is
blood relationship. The direct line of consanguinity consists of
all direct ancestors (parents, grandparents, great-grand-
parents, etc.) and all direct descendants (children, grand-
children, great-grandchildren, etc.). The collateral line consists of brothers and sisters; aunts and uncles, great-aunts and
great-uncles, etc.; nephews and nieces, great-nephews and
great-nieces, etc.; first cousins, second cousins, third cousins,
etc. Affinity is the relationship established by a valid marriage, commonly known as the in-law relationship. For example, canon law refers to the relationship between a man and his
mother-in-law as that of affinity in the first degree of the direct
line. The degree of relationship is computed according to the
rules of c. 108. N.B. This system is different from that of the
former law.

## Adopted Children

Canon 110. Children who are adopted according to
the norm of civil law are considered to be the children of the person or persons who adopted them.

## Membership in a Rite

Canon 111,1. If both parents belong to the Latin
church, their child becomes a member of that church

by receiving baptism in it. If one of them does not belong to the Latin church, they may decide by common agreement to have their child baptized in the Latin church; but if they are unable to agree, the child should become a member of the ritual church to which the father belongs.

2. Anyone being baptized who is at least 14 may freely choose to be baptized in the Latin church or in some other ritual church. In such a case the person belongs to that church which he/she chooses.

## Transfer of Rite

Canon 112,1. After baptism one can become a member of another ritual church if one:

1) obtains the permission of the Apostolic See;

2) is a spouse who, when getting married or during the marriage, declares that he/she is transferring to the ritual church of the other spouse; if the marriage is dissolved, however, he/she may freely return to the Latin church; or

3) is a child under 14 of those mentioned in nn. 1 or 2; or in a mixed marriage is a child under 14 of the Catholic party who has legitimately transferred to another ritual church; but when the children become 14 or older they may choose to return to the Latin church.

2. The practice, however long, of receiving the sacraments according to the rite of another ritual church does not bring about membership in that church.

## Juridic Persons

Canon 113,2. Besides physical persons there are also juridic persons in the Church, that is, subjects in canon law of obligations and rights which are congruent with their nature.

A juridic person, formerly called a moral person, is an aggregate of persons or things. For example, a religious institute of priests and brothers is a juridic person which is an aggregate of persons. The institute itself is the juridic person, the legal entity; the actual members of the institute are physical persons, the priests and brothers. A trust fund for seminarian scholarships is an example of a juridic person which is an aggregate of things, namely, of stocks, money, or other assets. Other examples of juridic persons are the Apostolic See, a diocese, a parish, a Catholic organization. Juridic persons must be legally established according to the norm of law. Further norms are found in cc. 114–123.

## Power of Governance

Canon 129,2. The laity are able to cooperate in the exercise of the power of governance according to the norm of law.

In the old law the power of governance was usually called the power of jurisdiction. The 1917 Code restricted the exercise of this power to clerics alone. An important development toward conceding the capability of laypersons to exercise the power of governance occurred in 1971 when Pope Paul VI allowed laymen to serve as judges in church courts under certain conditions. This canon recognizes that laypersons are able to exercise ecclesiastical governance, and the Code provides certain ways in which this can be done. For example, both lay men and women may now serve as tribunal judges in certain circumstances. This is an example of the judicial power of governance. The power of governance is divided into legislative, executive, and judicial branches. Only bishops may exercise legislative power.

# Book II
# The People of God

Book II is the longest book of the Code consisting of 543 canons. It is divided into three parts: (1) the faithful, (2) the hierarchical constitution of the Church, and (3) institutes of consecrated life and societies of apostolic life. The initial sections of Part I on the faithful (cc.204–231) treat fundamental doctrine, rights, and discipline common to all the faithful. One section is exclusively devoted to the rights and obligations of the laity. There are also certain canons from Part II on the hierarchical ordering of the Church which are of interest to a general Catholic audience, especially those which define the many structures, offices, and ministries open to lay participation.

*The Faithful*

Canon 204,1. The faithful are those who, inasmuch as they have been incorporated in Christ by bap-

> tism, are constituted the people of God. For this rea-
> son they have been made sharers in their own way
> in the priestly, prophetic, and kingly functions of
> Christ. According to their own proper condition,
> they are called to exercise the mission which God
> has entrusted the Church to fulfill in the world.
> 2. This Church, which is established and ordered in
> this world as a society, subsists in the Catholic
> Church, governed by the successor of Peter and the
> bishops in communion with him.

This canon defines the faithful (*christifideles*) as all the baptized. However, the scope of the Code is restricted to Catholics
of the Latin rite. For the most part the term "faithful" should
be understood and applied in this restricted meaning unless in
a particular canon the broader understanding is evident. This
canon is an example of the broader meaning given "the faithful." All the baptized, Catholics and non-Catholics, make up
the people of God. They share the threefold functions of Christ
who is priest, prophet, and king. Christ entrusted these same
functions to his Church. The structure of the Code reflects
these functions or duties: Book III treats the teaching function
of the Church (Christ as prophet); Book IV takes up the sanctifying function of the Church (Christ as priest); and the governance function is promoted by the entire Code (Christ as king).
C. 204,2 notes the unique role the Catholic Church enjoys
among the people of God.

## Full Communion with the Catholic Church

> Canon 205. Those who are fully in communion with
> the Catholic Church here on earth are those bap-
> tized who are united with Christ to the Church's
> visible structure by the bonds of the profession of
> faith, the sacraments, and ecclesiastical governance.

Those who are in full communion with the Church are called Roman Catholics, or simply Catholics, whether they belong to the Latin rite or to one of the eastern rites. Protestants, Orthodox, and other baptized non-Catholics are not in full communion because they lack one or more of the three essential elements of unity: the profession of faith, the sacraments, and ecclesiastical governance.

## Catechumens

> Canon 206,1. Catechumens are associated to the Church in a special way. Moved by the Holy Spirit, they explicitly desire to be incorporated into the Church and therefore by that very desire, as well as by a life of faith, hope, and charity, they are joined with the Church which already considers them as her own.
>
> 2. The Church has a special care for catechumens. It invites them to pursue the evangelical life and introduces them to the celebration of the sacred rites, and it already grants them various prerogatives which are enjoyed by Christians.

A catechumen is a person who has been admitted by the Church into the catechumenate, which is a period of preparation for the reception of the sacraments of initiation—baptism, confirmation, and Eucharist. Although catechumens are not yet baptized and therefore are not members of the Church, their very desire to be baptized gives them a special status in the Church which entitles them to certain prerogatives such as the right to ecclesiastical funeral rites.

## Clergy, Laity, Religious

> Canon 207,1. Among the faithful in the Church there are, by divine institution, ordained ministers

who also are called clerics in the law; the other
members of the faithful are called the laity.
2. Among both clerics and laity there are those
members of the faithful who are consecrated to God
in a special way and who promote the salvific mission of the Church. These persons profess the evan-
gelical counsels by vows or other sacred bonds which
are recognized and sanctioned by the Church. Although their status is not part of the hierarchical
structure of the Church, they nevertheless belong to
its life and holiness.

The Church teaches that the role of ordained ministry in the
Church is part of God's plan. Ordained ministers are also
called clerics to distinguish them from other members of the
faithful who are called laity or laypersons. There are three
orders of clerics: deacons, priests, and bishops. C. 207,2 speaks
of those members of the faithful who are consecrated to God in
a special way. The Church recognizes four kinds of consecrated
life: religious institutes, secular institutes, hermits, and vir-
gins. Also in the Church there are societies of apostolic life
which are associations of faithful who do not profess vows but
are joined together by a common commitment to promote various forms of apostolic service, such as foreign missionary work.
The Code treats these groups in Part III of Book II.

# The Obligations and Rights of all the Faithful

This section and the following one on the obligations and
rights of the laity are both new to the revised Code. These new
sections reflect the contemporary Church's greater concern for
the rights and equality of all its members. They also witness to
the greater role of lay people in the Church today and recognize their unique status and special contributions to the
Church.

## Equality of the Faithful

Canon 208. By their rebirth in Christ all the faithful are equal in dignity and action. As a result, they all cooperate in building up the body of Christ according to their own proper condition and function.

## Observance of Communion

Canon 209,1. The faithful are obliged always to observe communion with the Church, even in their external actions.

## Fulfillment of Duties

Canon 209,2. The faithful should fulfill diligently their responsibilities to both the universal Church and the particular church to which by law they belong.

## Spiritual Duties

Canon 210. All the faithful, according to their proper condition, must use their energies to lead a holy life and to promote the growth of the Church and its continuous sanctification.

## Evangelization

Canon 211. All the faithful have the duty and the right to work for the ever-increasing spread of the divine message of salvation to all people of all times in every part of the world.

## Obedience to Church Authority

Canon 212,1. Conscious of their own responsibilities, the faithful are bound in Christian obedience to follow whatever Church authorities, as representatives of Christ, declare as teachers of the faith or decree as leaders of the Church.

## Freedom of Petition

Canon 212,2. The faithful are at liberty to make their needs known to ecclesiastical authorities, especially spiritual needs, and to make known their desires.

## Expression of Opinions

Canon 212,3. In virtue of the knowledge, competence, and expertise which they may have, the faithful have the right and sometimes even the duty to make known their own opinion to Church authorities about those things which pertain to the good of the Church. Without prejudice to the integrity of faith and morals and with respect for Church authorities, and attentive to the common good and the dignity of persons, they also have the right to express their opinions to other members of the faithful.

## Word and Sacrament

Canon 213. The faithful have the right to receive from Church authorities assistance from the spiritual goods of the Church, especially the word of God and the sacraments.

## Worship and Spirituality

Canon 214. The faithful have the right to participate in the worship of God according to their own rite approved by legitimate ecclesiastical authorities. They also have the right to follow their own form of spirituality, provided it is consonant with Church doctrine.

## Associations and Meetings

Canon 215. The faithful are at liberty freely to establish and conduct associations for the purposes of charity or piety, or to foster the Christian vocation in the world. They are free to hold meetings in order to pursue these ends in common.

## Promotion of the Apostolate

Canon 216. Because they participate in the mission of the Church, all the faithful have the right, even on their own initiative, to promote or sustain the apostolate according to their own status and condition. However, the name "Catholic" may not be given to any project without the consent of the competent ecclesiastical authority.

## Christian Education

Canon 217. Since they are called by baptism to lead a life in harmony with the teaching of the gospel, the faithful have the right to Christian education, by which they are properly instructed to acquire maturity as human persons and likewise to know and live the mystery of salvation.

## Academic Freedom

Canon 218. Those who are engaged in sacred disciplines enjoy a just freedom of inquiry and of prudently expressing their views on matters in which they are competent while observing compliance due to the magisterium of the Church.

## Freedom of Vocational Choice

Canon 219. All the faithful have the right to be immune from any force in choosing their state in life.

## Good Reputation and Privacy

Canon 220. No one may illegitimately harm someone's good reputation, nor violate the right of each person to protect his or her own privacy.

## Procedural Rights

Canon 221,1. It is within the competence of all the faithful legitimately to vindicate and defend their ecclesial rights in the competent ecclesiastical forum according to the norm of law.
2. If they are called to judgment by competent authority, the faithful also have the right to be judged according to the prescriptions of the law applied with equity.
3. The faithful have the right not to be punished by canonical penalties unless this is done according to the norm of law.

## Support of the Church

Canon 222,1. The faithful are obliged to provide for the needs of the Church in order to make available those things which are necessary for divine worship, for works of the apostolate and of charity, and for the support of the Church's ministers.

## Social Justice

Canon 222,2. The faithful are obliged to promote social justice, mindful of the command of the Lord to support the poor from one's own resources.

## Limitations on Rights

Canon 223,1. In the exercise of their rights the faithful, both individually and joined together in associations, must take into account the common good of the Church, the rights of others, and their own duties towards others.
2. Ecclesiastical authority is competent, in virtue of the common good, to moderate the exercise of the rights belonging to the faithful.

# The Obligations and Rights of the Laity

Canon 224. Besides having the obligations and rights which are common to all the faithful and those given elsewhere in the canons, the laity are also bound to the obligations and enjoy the rights which are specified in this section.

## Evangelization

Canon 225,1. Just as all members of the faithful are deputed for the apostolate by God through baptism and confirmation, the laity too are bound by obligation and they enjoy the right, both individually and collectively, to work so that the divine message of salvation be known and accepted by all people everywhere on the earth. This obligation is all the more urgent in those circumstances in which people are unable to hear the gospel and to learn about Christ except through laypersons.

2. The laity are bound by the special duty, according to their proper condition, to imbue and perfect the temporal order with the spirit of the gospel. In carrying out these matters and in pursuing secular functions in such a way, they provide a unique kind of witness to Christ.

## Married Persons

Canon 226,1. In accord with their proper vocation, married persons have a special duty to work to build up the people of God by their marriage and family.

2. Since they have brought life to their children, parents are bound by a serious obligation and they enjoy the right to educate their children. It is a primary task of Christian parents to ensure the Christian education of their children according to the teachings handed down by the Church.

## Civil Liberties

Canon 227. The laity have the right to all civil liberties that other citizens enjoy. Nevertheless, in using these liberties they should take care that their actions are imbued with the spirit of the gospel, and that they take into account the teachings proposed by the Church's magisterium. Moreover, on debatable issues they should beware of proposing their own opinions as being the teaching of the Church.

## Capability for Ministry

Canon 228,1. Laypersons who are deemed suitable may be chosen by Church authorities for those

Church offices and functions which they are capable
of having according to the law.

## Lay Experts at Church Councils

Canon 228,2. Laypersons who excel in the necessary knowledge, prudence, and integrity are capable
of serving as experts or advisors to the authorities of
the Church, including councils, according to the
norm of law.

The Church has various kinds of councils: the ecumenical
council for the universal Church, such as Vatican II; plenary
councils, which are held for an entire region of an episcopal
conference, such as that of the United States; and provincial
councils for ecclesiastical provinces composed of all the dioceses in a territory under the leadership of a single arch-
diocese. Only bishops can make laws for the Church, but other
members of the faithful can be called to Church councils in an
advisory capacity. C. 443 treats the membership of plenary and
provincial councils, including the consultive role of select
laypersons.

## Knowledge of Doctrine

Canon 229,1. Laypersons are bound by obligation
and enjoy the right to acquire a knowledge of Christian doctrine appropriate to their capacity and condition so that they may be able to live according to
it, to make it known, to defend it if necessary, and to
have their own proper role in the exercise of the
apostolate.
2. Laypersons also enjoy the right to acquire a deep-
er knowledge of the sacred sciences which are
taught at ecclesiastical universities and faculties or
in institutes of religious studies by attending lec-
tures and pursuing academic degrees.

The sacred sciences include the various theological disciplines and canon law. Many graduate schools of theology and even some Catholic seminaries encourage laypersons to pursue both academic degrees and professional ministerial degrees.

## Mandate to Teach Sacred Sciences

> Canon 229,3. If they meet all the prescribed requirements, laypersons are capable of receiving from the legitimate ecclesiastical authority a mandate to teach the sacred sciences.

C. 812 requires that all those who teach theological disciplines in any institutes of higher studies must have a mandate from the competent ecclesiastical authority.

## Liturgical Ministries

> Canon 230,1. Lay men, who are of the age and possess the qualities required by the episcopal conference, are able to take on the permanent ministries of lector or acolyte in accord with the prescribed liturgical rites. However, the conferral of these ministries does not grant the right to receive support or remuneration from the Church.
> 2. Laypersons are able to fulfill the function of lector during the liturgy by means of a temporary deputation. Likewise, all the laity are able to function as commentators, cantors, and other ministries according to the norm of law.
> 3. When the needs of the Church warrant it and when ministers are lacking, the laity, even if they are not lectors or acolytes, are able to fulfill some of their duties, namely, to exercise the ministry of the word, to preside over liturgical prayers, to confer baptism, and to distribute Holy Communion, observing the prescriptions of the law.

The *permanent* ministries of acolyte and lector are the only lay ministries mentioned in the Code which are not open to women. The reason is likely that these ministries are steps on the way to holy orders.

## Formation for Ministry

> Canon 231,1. The laity, who either permanently or for a certain period of time are devoted to some special service of the Church, are obliged to acquire a fitting formation needed to fulfill their function properly, and they are obliged to carry out this function conscientiously, earnestly, and diligently.

## Wages and Benefits

> Canon 231,2. With the exception mentioned in c. 230,1, laypersons have a right to an honest remuneration suitable to their condition so that they might be able to provide decently for their own needs and those of their family. The civil laws should also be observed in this matter. Likewise, lay people have the right that their insurance, social security, and health benefits be duly provided for.

# Associations of the Faithful

> Canon 298,1. There are associations in the Church, distinct from institutes of consecrated life and societies of apostolic life, composed of the faithful whether cleric, or lay, or cleric and lay together. The members of these associations strive through common works to foster a more perfect life, or to promote public worship or Christian doctrine, or other works of the apostolate, namely, evangelization, works of

piety or charity, and the animation of the temporal
order with the Christian spirit.

The freedom of the faithful to form associations is stated in c.
215. Examples of associations are third orders, the Knights of
Columbus, and the Confraternity of Christian Doctrine. No
association can be called "Catholic" without the consent of the
competent ecclesiastical authority who must also approve the
statutes of such an association. Associations of the faithful
which are erected by competent ecclesiastical authority are
called public associations. Those which are formed by the faithful themselves are called private associations. A private association must have its statutes reviewed by competent ecclesiastical authority in order to be recognized as an association of
the faithful. The norms for associations are found in cc.
298–329. Cc. 327–329 are special norms on lay associations in
particular. Personal prelatures, such as Opus Dei, are not governed by the canons on associations but are treated separately
in cc. 294–297.

# The Hierarchical Constitution of the Church

This section of the Code (cc. 330–572) treats the organization
of the Church on the universal and local levels. Some canons
are of particular relevance to the laity, especially those on the
many structures and offices which are open to lay involvement.
We have already seen certain ministries which qualified
laypersons may exercise (cc. 228–230), and other ministries
and offices are treated elsewhere in the Code, notably in Books
III, IV, and VII. In this section of the Code, the structures and
offices open to the laity are mainly those of administration and
pastoral care on the diocesan and parish levels.

## The Diocesan Synod

> Canon 460. The diocesan synod is a group of se-
> lected priests and other members of the faithful of a
> particular church who offer assistance to the di-
> ocesan bishop for the good of the entire diocesan
> community according to the norm of the following
> canons.

C. 368 lists various kinds of "particular churches," but the
diocese is the most common. A chief purpose of the diocesan
synod is to assist the bishop in preparing legislation for the
diocese. The bishop is the only legislator in the diocesan synod,
and the other members have only consultive vote. Nevertheless, the synod can be a very important and effective means for
wide-ranging consultation and action on many matters that
affect the life of the diocese. Among those who must participate
in the diocesan synod are members of the laity chosen by the
pastoral council in a way and in numbers determined by the
bishop. Where there is no pastoral council, the matter is determined by the bishop. The canonical regulations governing the
diocesan synod are found in cc. 461–468.

## The Diocesan Curia

> Canon 469. The diocesan curia consists of those in-
> stitutions and persons offering assistance to the
> bishop in the governance of the whole diocese, es-
> pecially in directing pastoral action, in caring for
> the administration of the diocese, and in exercising
> judicial power.

The diocesan curia is the collective name for all the pastoral,
administrative, and judicial offices of a diocese. The judicial
offices are treated in Book VII on procedures. Pastoral and
administrative structures vary according to the needs and de-

sires of local churches, but some specific ones are required by law. Among these the offices open to laypersons are the chancellor, vice-chancellor, notary, finance council member, and financial officer.

## Chancellor

> Canon 482,1. In every curia a chancellor is appointed whose principal duty, unless otherwise stated in particular law, is to see that the acts of the curia are collected and organized, and kept in the curial archives.

## Vice-chancellor

> Canon 482,2. If it seems necessary, the chancellor may be given an assistant who is called a vice-chancellor.

## Notary

> Canon 482,3. The chancellor and vice-chancellor are themselves notaries or secretaries of the curia.
> Canon 483,1. Besides the chancellor, other notaries may be appointed whose signature establishes the authenticity of all acts, including judicial acts or the acts of certain causes or transactions.

Further norms on the chancellor, vice-chancellor, and notary are found in cc. 483,2–491.

## Finance Council

> Canon 492,1. Each diocese should have a finance council headed by the diocesan bishop or his delegate and consisting of at least three members of the

faithful named by the bishop. They must be truly competent in economic matters and in civil law, and have outstanding integrity.

2. The members of the finance council serve a five-year term, but they may be reappointed to further terms.

3. Those who are related to the bishop up to the fourth degree of consanguinity or affinity are not eligible for the finance council.

The fourth degree of consanguinity in the collateral line is the relationship between first cousins. Fourth degree affinity is the relationship with the spouse of one's first cousin. C. 493 treats the duties of the finance council, notably the preparation of the annual budget and the approval of the annual financial report.

## Financial Officer

Canon 494,1. After consulting with the college of consultors and with the finance council, the bishop in every diocese shall appoint a financial officer who is truly competent in economic matters and who has outstanding integrity.

The other paragraphs of this canon specify the term of office and duties of the financial officer which are similar to those of the financial council.

## Pastoral Council

Canon 511. Insofar as pastoral circumstances recommend it, a pastoral council should be established in every diocese. The pastoral council, under the authority of the bishop, has the task of investigating those matters pertaining to pastoral work in the di-

ocese, to ponder them, and to propose practical
conclusions.

The pastoral council consists of both lay and clerical members of the faithful chosen in a manner determined by the
bishop. The various regions, social conditions, professions, and
apostolates in the diocese should be represented on the pastoral council. The body meets at least once a year for a duration
determined by the bishop. Like the diocesan synod, the pastoral council has only consultive vote. The norms governing
pastoral councils are found in cc. 512–514.

## Shared Parochial Ministry

> Canon 517,2. Due to a scarcity of priests, the di-
> ocesan bishop may entrust deacons or laypersons or
> a community of persons with a share in the exercise
> of the pastoral care of a parish. However, some
> priest endowed with the powers and faculties of the
> pastor should be appointed to moderate the pastoral
> care.

This canon allows for many possibilities for lay leadership in
parishes, including team ministry or even laypersons as "administrators" of parishes which do not have a resident, functioning priest.

## Parish Council

> Canon 536,1. After consulting the priests' senate, if
> the diocesan bishop judges it opportune, a pastoral
> council should be established in each parish. It is
> composed of the pastor who presides over it and
> other faithful along with those who by virtue of of-
> fice are part of the pastoral effort of the parish. The
> council offers assistance in fostering pastoral action.

2. The pastoral council has a consultive vote only and is regulated by norms established by the diocesan bishop.

## Parish Financial Affairs Council

Canon 537. Each parish should have a financial affairs council which is governed by universal law and the norms of the diocesan bishop. The members of the council, selected according to these norms, assist the pastor in the financial administration of the parish, without prejudice to c. 532.

C. 532 states that the pastor represents the parish in all juridic affairs.

# Book III
# The Teaching Function of the Church

Christ was a prophet and teacher, called "rabbi" by his disciples, and he entrusted to his Church the function of teaching the gospel to all nations. The Church carries on the prophetic mission of Christ by its preaching, catechetical instruction, missionary activity, Catholic education, and by making use of instruments of social communication, especially books. Book III of the Code of Canon Law establishes regulations for all these means of teaching. Although it is a relatively short book of only 87 canons (cc. 747–833), there is much of importance contained herein since all Catholics have their own role to play in the Church's teaching function.

## Freedom of Religion

Canon 748,1. All persons are bound to seek the truth in those matters which pertain to God and his

Church. They are bound by divine law and they enjoy the right to embrace and to observe that truth which they acknowledge.

2. No one may ever force people to embrace the Catholic faith against their conscience.

## Divine Revelation

Canon 750. By divine and Catholic faith, all those things must be believed which are contained in the word of God, whether in scripture or tradition, that is, those things which are contained in the one deposit of faith entrusted to the Church. These matters are proposed as divinely revealed either by the solemn magisterium of the Church or by its ordinary and universal magisterium. This is manifest by the common adherence to these truths by the faithful under the guidance of the sacred magisterium. Therefore all are bound to avoid contrary teachings.

## Heresy, Apostasy, Schism

Canon 751. Heresy is the obstinate denial after the reception of baptism of some truth which must be believed as divine and Catholic faith, or it is an obstinate doubt about the same. Apostasy is the total repudiation of the Christian faith after baptism. Schism is the refusal after baptism to submit to the Roman pontiff or to reject communion with the members of the Church subject to him.

## Respect for the Magisterium

Canon 752. A religious respect of intellect and will, even if not the assent of faith, must be given to the teachings of the supreme pontiff or the college of bishops on matters of faith or morals when they exercise the authentic magisterium, even if they do not intend to proclaim it by a definitive act. Therefore the faithful should take care to avoid whatever is not in harmony with this.

## Bishops as Authentic Teachers

Canon 753. The bishops who are in communion with the head and members of the college of bishops are authentic doctors and teachers of the faith whether they act individually or are gathered in an episcopal conference or a particular council. Although bishops do not enjoy infallibility in such cases, the faithful, with a spirit of religious respect, are bound to observe the authentic teaching of their bishops.

## Obedience to the Magisterium

Canon 754. All the faithful are bound to observe the constitutions and decrees which the legitimate authority of the Church issues in order to explain doctrine or to denounce erroneous opinions. This refers especially to those constitutions and decrees issued by the Roman pontiff or the college of bishops.

# The Ministry of the Divine Word

## Role of the Laity

Canon 759. Lay members of the faithful, by virtue of their baptism and confirmation, are witnesses to the gospel message in word and by the example of their Christian lives. They may also be called to

> share with the bishop and the priests in the exercise
> of the ministry of the word.

The Code sees the ministry of God's word exercised principally by preaching and by catechetical formation. Other means include teaching in schools and academies, holding conferences and meetings, and making use of the press and other means of social communication. The ministry of the divine word seeks to impart the mysteries of Christ which are grounded in scripture, tradition, the liturgy, and the magisterium and life of the Church. Cc. 756–761 give general norms on this ministry.

## Lay Preaching

> Canon 766. Lay persons may be allowed to preach in a church or oratory if in certain circumstances need requires it or in particular cases utility recommends it. This may be done in accord with the prescriptions of the episcopal conference and without prejudice to c. 767,1.

C. 767,1 states that the homily in the liturgy is reserved to the priest or deacon.

## Catechetical Instruction

> Canon 773. There is a proper and serious duty, especially on the part of pastoral ministers, to provide catechesis for the Christian people so that the faith of believers becomes living, manifest, and fruitful as a result of formation in Church teaching and experience in Christian living.
> Canon 774,1. Under the guidance of legitimate ecclesiastical authority, the Church's concern for catechesis is extended to all members according to each one's own role.

## Role of Parents in Religious Formation

Canon 774,2. Parents above all are obliged in word and example to form their children in faith and in the practice of the Christian life. Godparents and those who take the place of parents are bound by this same obligation.

## Role of Others in Religious Formation

Canon 776. In virtue of his office the pastor is bound to provide for the catechetical formation of adults, young people, and children. For this purpose he should make use of the assistance of other clerics in the parish; of members of institutes of consecrated life and societies of apostolic life, keeping in mind the proper character of each institute; and also of the lay faithful, especially religious educators. None of these should refuse to give assistance readily unless they have a legitimate excuse. The pastor should also promote and foster the duty of parents to provide family catechesis as was stated in c. 774,2.

## Means of Religious Education

Canon 779. Catechetical formation should be given by using all means of assistance, teaching aids, and means of social communication which seem more effective in enabling the faithful, according to their character, talents, age, and condition in life to learn Catholic teaching more thoroughly and be prepared to put it into practice.

## Formation of Religious Educators

Canon 780. Local ordinaries should see to it that religious educators are prepared fittingly for the proper execution of their task, namely, that an on-going formation be offered them so that they can fully know the teachings of the Church and learn both theoretically and practically the proper tools of religious education.

# The Missionary Activity of the Church

Canon 781. Since the whole Church is missionary by nature and evangelization is a fundamental duty of the people of God, all the faithful, conscious of their own responsibility, should assume their own part in missionary work.

## Missionaries

Canon 784. Missionaries are those who are sent by competent ecclesiastical authority to do missionary work. They may or may not be native to the mission land. They may be secular clergy, members of institutes of consecrated life or of societies of apostolic life, or they may be lay members of the faithful.

## Catechists

Canon 785,1. Catechists should be engaged to pursue missionary work. Catechists are lay members of the faithful who are suitably instructed and who are excellent Christians. Their task is to explain the teaching of the gospel and to organize liturgical services and charitable works under the moderation of the missionary.

2. Catechists should be formed in schools designated for this purpose or, where these schools are lacking, under the moderation of the missionaries.

## First World Responsibilities

Canon 791. In order to promote missionary cooperation in every diocese:
1) missionary vocations should be fostered;
2) a priest should be appointed to promote effectively all efforts on behalf of the missions, especially the *Pontifical Missionary Works;*
3) an annual mission day should be celebrated;
4) each year a fitting contribution to the missions
should be made and sent to the Holy See.

# Catholic Education

## Rights and Duties of Parents

Canon 793,1. Parents and those who take their
place are bound by obligation and enjoy the right to
educate their children. Catholic parents also have
the duty and right to choose those means and in-
stitutions by which, according to local circumstances, they are best able to provide for the Catholic education of their children.

## State Support of Catholic Education

Canon 793,2. It is also the right of parents to receive
the assistance furnished by civil society which is
needed for the Catholic education of their children.

## Aims of Catholic Education

Canon 795. A true education must strive for the entire formation of the human person, including a formation geared toward one's final goal as well as

toward the common good of society. Therefore, children and young people should be so reared that they are able to develop harmoniously their physical, moral, and intellectual endowments; that they may acquire a better sense of responsibility and a correct use of freedom; and that they are able to take on an active role in social life.

## Schools

Canon 796,1. The faithful should value highly schools among the means of providing education. Schools are a principal help to parents in fulfilling their task of education.

## Parent/Teacher Cooperation

Canon 796,2. Parents must closely cooperate with school teachers to whom they entrust their children's education. In fulfilling their duty the teachers should closely collaborate with parents. They should willingly listen to parents and should have associations or meetings for them which should be highly esteemed.

## Freedom to Choose Schools

Canon 797. It is necessary that parents enjoy true freedom in choosing schools. The faithful must be sollicitous so that the civil society recognizes this freedom of parents and, observing distributive justice, also safeguards it with its assistance.

## Preference for Catholic Schools

Canon 798. Parents should enroll their children in those schools where a Catholic education is provided. If they are unable to do this, they are bound to see that a fitting Catholic education is provided outside the school.

## Religious Education in Public Schools

Canon 799. The faithful should seek to have the civil laws on the education of youth include provisions for religious and moral education in the schools themselves, in accord with the parents' conscience.

## Support of Catholic Schools

Canon 800,1. The Church has the right to found and run schools of any discipline, kind, and grade whatsoever.
2. The faithful, according to their means, should foster Catholic schools by helping to found them and maintain them.

## Approval of Religion Teachers

Canon 805. For his own diocese the local ordinary has the right to appoint or approve religion teachers. He may also remove them or demand that they be removed for reasons of religion or morals.

## Duty of Catholic School Principals

Canon 806,2. The directors of Catholic schools, under the vigilance of the local ordinary, should ensure that their institution provides instruction at least equal on an academic level to that of other schools in the region.

## Teachers at Catholic Universities

Canon 810,1. That authority who is competent according to the statutes of the institution has the duty to ensure that the teachers who are appointed to Catholic universities are not only academically and pedagogically competent but also excel in doctrinal integrity and probity of life. If these requisites are deficient the teachers may be removed, observing the proper procedures defined in the statutes.
2. The appropriate conferences of bishops and diocesan bishops have the duty and the right to be vigilant so that in universities the principles of Catholic doctrine are faithfully observed.

## Mandate to Teach Theology

Canon 812. Whoever teaches theological disciplines in any institute of higher studies whatsoever must have a mandate from the competent ecclesiastical authority.

## Campus Ministry

Canon 813. The diocesan bishop should provide significant pastoral care for university students, even by erecting a parish for them, or at least by appointing priests for them on a stable basis. The bishop should provide universities, even non-Catholic ones, with Catholic centers which furnish assistance to students, especially spiritual assistance.

## Ecclesiastical Universities and Faculties

Canon 819. Insofar as it is required for the good of a diocese or of a religious institute or of the universal

Church, diocesan bishops or the competent superior of institutes must send to ecclesiastical universities or faculties young people, clerics, or members of the institutes who are outstanding in character, virtue, and talent.

# Means of Social Communication, Especially Books

Canon 822,1. Ecclesiastical authorities should make use of the various means of social communication. This is a right which the Church has in order to fulfill its function.

2. These authorities should ensure that the faithful are taught of their duty to cooperate so that use of the means of social communication is animated by a human and Christian spirit.

3. All the faithful, especially those who are involved in any way in the regulation or use of the various media, should be solicitous in assisting the Church's pastoral activity so that the Church may exercise its function more effectively through the use of the media.

## Church Vigilance over Media

Canon 823,1. In order that the integrity of the truths of the faith and of morals be preserved, it is the duty and right of ecclesiastical authorities to be vigilant lest the faith or morals of the faithful be harmed by writings or by the use of means of social communication. Likewise, ecclesiastical authorities have the duty and right to require that the writings of the faithful which treat issues of faith or morals be subjected to their judgment before publication,

and to disapprove of those which harm correct faith
or good morals.

## Ecclesiastical Permission to Publish

Canon 824,1. Unless otherwise stated, the local ordinary whose permission or approval must be obtained for publishing books, according to the canons
of this section, is the proper local ordinary of the
author or the ordinary of the place in which the
books are being published.
2. Unless otherwise evident, whatever is said in this
title concerning books must be applied to any writings destined for public distribution.

## Catechisms

Canon 827,1. Catechisms and other writings deal-
ing with catechetical instruction, or their transla-
tions, require approval by the local ordinary before
publication, without prejudice to c. 775,2.

C. 775,2 states that episcopal conferences may publish catechisms for their territory which have the previous approval of
the Apostolic See.

## Textbooks

Canon 827,2. The competent ecclesiastical authority must approve before or after publication all text-
books for use in elementary, middle, or superior
schools which treat questions on the following subjects: sacred scripture, theology, canon law, church
history, and religious and moral disciplines.

## Books on Religious Topics

Canon 827,3. It is recommended that books treating
matters referred to in c. 827,2, even though they are

not used as instructional texts, should be subjected to the judgment of the local ordinary. This is also true of any writings which are particularly concerned with religion or morals.

## Distribution of Books in Churches

Canon 827,4. Books or other writings treating questions of religion or morals may not be displayed, sold, or distributed in churches or oratories unless they have been published with the permission of the competent ecclesiastical authority or they have afterwards been approved by him.

## Anti-Catholic Publications

Canon 831,1. Unless they have a just and reasonable cause, the faithful should not write anything in those newspapers, magazines, or journals which are accustomed manifestly to attack the Catholic religion or good morals. Moreover, clergy and members of religious institutes may not do so unless they have permission of the local ordinary.

# Book IV
# The Sanctifying Function of the Church

Christ the priest entrusted to his Church the function of sanctifying, of making people holy. The Church exercises its sanctifying function in a special way through its liturgical and sacramental life. Other means and actions of sanctification include its prayer life and acts of penance and charity. Book IV of the Code, the second largest book with 420 canons, is divided into three parts: (1) the sacraments, (2) other acts of divine worship, and (3) sacred places and times. Because the Church's sanctifying function so directly affects and involves all the people of God, it is not surprising that a large number of canons from Book IV is applicable to all Catholics, and some canons are of special pertinence to the laity.

*The Sacred Liturgy*

Canon 834,1. The Church fulfills its sanctifying function in a special way through the sacred liturgy,

which is indeed considered to be an exercise of the
priestly function of Jesus Christ. In the liturgy the
sanctification of men and women is signified by sen-
sible signs and is effected in a way proper to each
sign. In the liturgy the public worship of God is exercised integrally by the mystical body of Jesus Christ,
namely, by its head and its members.
2. This kind of worship exists when it is carried out
in the name of the Church by legitimately deputed
persons and through actions approved by the authority of the Church.

## Role of Laity, Parents

Canon 835,4. Lay members of the faithful have
their own role in the Church's sanctifying function
by actively participating in their own way in liturgical celebrations, especially the Eucharist. In a special way parents participate in this same function by
leading their conjugal life in a Christian spirit and
by providing a Christian education for their
children.

## Variety of Roles and Ministries

Canon 837,1. Liturgical actions are not private actions but celebrations of the Church itself which is
the "sacrament of unity," a holy people joined under
the bishops and directed by them. Thus the liturgy
pertains to the whole body of the Church and man-
ifests it and affects it. The individual members of the
Church relate to the liturgy in various ways according to the diversity of orders, functions, and actual
participation.

## Communal Nature of the Liturgy

Canon 837,2. By their very nature liturgical actions
imply communal celebration, and therefore they

should be celebrated whenever possible with the attendance and active participation of the faithful.

### Prayer, Penance, Charity

Canon 839,1. The Church also carries out its sanctifying function by other means, namely, by prayers by which it asks God that the faithful be made holy in the truth; and by works of penance and charity which indeed contribute greatly to the planting and strengthening of the kingdom of Christ in souls and which contribute to the welfare of the world.
2. Local ordinaries should ensure that the prayers and pious and sacred exercises of the Christian people are fully in harmony with the norms of the Church.

# Part I
# The Sacraments

Canon 840. The sacraments of the New Testament were instituted by Christ the Lord and entrusted to the Church. Insofar as they are actions of Christ and the Church, they are signs and means by which faith is expressed and strengthened, worship is given to God, and the sanctification of men and women is brought about. Therefore they contribute exceedingly to inducing, strengthening, and manifesting ecclesiastical communion. For these reasons, both ordained ministers and other members of the faithful must have the highest veneration and necessary diligence in the celebration of the sacraments.

## Christian Initiation

Canon 842,1. No one may validly be admitted to the other sacraments without having first received baptism.

2. The sacraments of baptism, confirmation, and Eucharist are so related to each other that all are required for full Christian initiation.

## Preparation for the Sacraments

Canon 843,1. Ordained ministers may not refuse the sacraments to those who ask for them under suitable circumstances, who are properly disposed, and who are not prohibited by law from receiving them.

2. Pastoral ministers and other members of the faithful, in accord with their position in the Church, have the duty to see that those who desire the sacraments are prepared to receive them through appropriate evangelization and catechetical formation in accord with the norms issued by competent authority.

## Reception of Sacraments by Catholics

Canon 844,1. Catholic ministers licitly administer the sacraments only to the Catholic faithful. Likewise, Catholics licitly receive them only from Catholic ministers. Exceptions are given in paragraphs 2, 3, and 4 of this canon and in c. 861,2.

2. As often as need requires it or true spiritual utility recommends it, and provided that the danger of error or indifference is avoided, the faithful for whom it is physically or morally impossible to go to a Catholic minister may receive the sacraments of

penance, Eucharist, and anointing of the sick from non-Catholic ministers of those churches in which these sacraments are valid.

The non-Catholic eastern churches, commonly called the Orthodox Church, is the main group of churches having sacraments recognized as valid by the Catholic Church. The sacraments of Protestant churches are not recognized as valid by the Catholic Church, except for the sacrament of baptism in many Protestant denominations.

## Administration of Sacraments to non-Catholics

Canon 844,3. Catholic ministers licitly administer the sacraments of penance, Eucharist, and anointing of the sick to members of the eastern churches which do not have full communion with the Catholic Church, if these persons spontaneously ask for the sacrament and are properly disposed. This also applies to members of other churches which, in the judgment of the Apostolic See, are in an equal condition to the eastern churches in reference to the sacraments.
4. If there is danger of death or, in the judgment of the diocesan bishop or the episcopal conference, there is some other serious need, Catholic ministers also licitly administer these same sacraments to other Christians who are not in full communion with the Catholic Church. This may be done when they are unable to go to a minister of their own community and they spontaneously ask for the sacrament, and provided they manifest the Catholic faith concerning these sacraments and are properly disposed.

## Conditional Administration of Sacraments

Canon 845,1. The sacraments of baptism, confirmation and orders cannot be repeated because they impart a character.
2. If after a diligent investigation there remains a prudent doubt whether the sacraments mentioned in paragraph one had been really or validly conferred, they should be conferred conditionally.

# Baptism

Canon 849. Baptism is the door to the sacraments and is necessary for salvation, at least the baptism of desire if not baptism with water. By baptism persons are freed from sin, recreated as children of God, conjoined to Christ by an indelible character, and incorporated into the Church. For validity, baptism must be conferred with real water using the proper words.

## Preparation for Baptism

Canon 851. The celebration of baptism must be fittingly prepared, and so:
1) An adult who intends to receive baptism should be admitted to the catechumenate and, as far as possible, should be gradually led to sacramental initiation through the various stages. This is to be done in accord with the rite of initiation adapted by the episcopal conference and in accord with the particular norms published by it.
2) The parents of an infant to be baptized, as well as those who will be the godparents, should be suitably instructed about the meaning of this sac-

rament and about the obligations that go with it. The pastor personally or through others should ensure that the parents are duly instructed through pastoral exhortations and even common prayer; several families may be brought together for this purpose and, where possible, each family visited.

## Adult and Infant Baptism

Canon 852,1. The prescriptions which in these canons refer to adult baptism are applicable to all who have left infancy and have attained the use of reason.
2. An infant, even in reference to baptism, includes anyone who is mentally incompetent (*non sui compos*).

Since canon law presumes that the use of reason is attained at age seven, ordinarily those seven and older should be baptized according to the *Rite of Christian Initiation of Adults* and therefore they should receive all three sacraments of initiation at the same ceremony.

## Immersion or Pouring

Canon 854. Baptism is conferred either by immersion in or by the pouring of water, observing the prescriptions of the episcopal conference.

## Name of Child

Canon 855. The parents, godparents, and pastor are to see that the name given is not foreign to Christian sentiment.

The canon does not require a saint's name, but only a name which is not offensive to Christians.

## Time of Baptism

Canon 856. Although baptism may be celebrated on any day, it is commendable to celebrate it ordinarily on Sundays or, if possible, at the Easter vigil.

## Place of Baptism

Canon 857,1. Except for cases of necessity, the proper place for baptism is a church or oratory.
2. As a rule adult baptism is given in one's parish church, infant baptism in the parents' parish church, unless there is just reason for having it in another church.

## Emergency Baptism in Home or Hospital

Canon 860,1. Except in a case of necessity, baptism should not be conferred in private homes, unless the local ordinary permits it for a serious reason.
2. Unless the diocesan bishop decreed something else, baptism should not be celebrated in hospitals except in a case of need or for some other cogent pastoral reason.

Sacraments are actions of the whole Church and not celebrations of private individuals or families. Therefore they should ordinarily be celebrated in church, especially baptism which is the sacrament of incorporation into the Church.

## Lay Ministers of Baptism

Canon 861,2. If the ordinary minister of baptism is absent or impeded, a catechist or someone else deputed for this task by the local ordinary may licitly confer baptism. In a case of necessity, anyone with the proper intention may baptize. Pastoral ministers, especially the pastor, should be solicitous in teaching the faithful the correct way to baptize.

The ordinary ministers of baptism are bishops, priests, and deacons. In addition, the local ordinary may appoint laypersons as special ministers of baptism who may baptize if the ordinary minister is not available. Anyone, even a non-believer, may baptize a person who is in danger of death if the one baptizing has the intention of doing what the Church does when it baptizes. The proper way to baptize in an emergency is to pour water on the person three times (or immerse) while saying the words, "I baptize you in the name of the Father, and of the Son, and of the Holy Spirit." If it is a conditional baptism, the words are: "If you are not baptized, I baptize you. . . ."

## Baptism by a Bishop

Canon 863. The baptism of adults, at least those who are 14 or older, should be referred to the diocesan bishop so that, if he judges it expedient, he himself may administer it.

In the early Church the local bishop administered all the sacraments, but as the Church grew this became impossible. This canon expresses the Church's desire to return to its ancient practice at least in part for adult initiates, especially those 14 and older.

## Capability for Baptism

Canon 864. Any person not yet baptized is capable of being baptized.

## Requirements for Adult Baptism

> Canon 865,1. For an adult to be baptized, he/she must manifest the desire to receive baptism, must be sufficiently instructed in the truths of the faith and the Christian obligations, and must be tested in the Christian life during the catechumenate. The one to be baptized should also be admonished to be sorry for his/her sins.
>
> 2. An adult in danger of death can be baptized if he/she has some knowledge of the principal truths of the faith, manifests in some way the intention to receive baptism, and promises to observe the requirements of the Christian religion.

## Requirements for Infant Baptism

> Canon 867,1. Parents are bound by obligation to see that their infants are baptized within the first weeks after birth. As soon as possible after birth, or even before it, they should see the pastor so that they may request the sacrament for their child and receive preparation for baptism.
>
> 2. If an infant is in danger of death, it should be baptized without delay.
>
> Canon 868,1. For an infant to be baptized licitly, it is necessary that:
>
> 1) at least one of the parents consent to it, or the person who lawfully takes their place consents;
>
> 2) there is a firm hope that the child will be educated in the Catholic religion; if this hope is really lacking, the baptism should be deferred according to the prescriptions of particular law, explaining the reason to the parents.
>
> 2. In danger of death the infant of Catholic parents, and even of non-Catholic parents, may be licitly baptized even if the parents are against it.

## Abandoned Infants

Canon 870. Unless after a diligent investigation its baptism has been proven, an abandoned infant or a foundling should be baptized.

## Aborted Fetuses

Canon 871. If they are living, aborted fetuses should be baptized insofar as possible.

## Godparents

Canon 872. There should be a godparent for the person to be baptized inasmuch as this is possible. In adult baptism the godparent assists the baptized in Christian initiation. In infant baptism the godparent, together with the parents, presents the child for baptism and helps the baptized to lead the Christian life expected by baptism and to fulfill faithfully the obligations inherent to it.

Canon 873. There may be one godfather, one godmother, or one of each.

## Requirements of Godparents

Canon 874,1. To be accepted to undertake the duty of a godparent, it is necessary:

1) that one be designated by the person to be baptized or by the parents or the person who takes their place or, if these are lacking, by the pastor or minister; and that one have the aptitude for and intention of carrying out this duty;

2) that one be at least 16, unless the diocesan bishop shall have established another age or unless in an exceptional case it seems to the pastor

or minister that there is just cause to admit a younger person;

3) that one is Catholic, confirmed, and already has received the Holy Eucharist, and likewise leads a life of faith in harmony with the undertaking of this duty;

4) that one is not under a lawfully imposed or declared canonical penalty;

5) that one is not the father or mother of the one to be baptized.

## Non-Catholic Witness

Canon 874,2. A baptized person belonging to a non-Catholic ecclesial community may be admitted as a witness to baptism but only along with a Catholic godparent.

A validly baptized Protestant or Orthodox, for example, may serve as a witness at Catholic baptism.

# Confirmation

Canon 879. The sacrament of confirmation imparts a character and enriches with the gift of the Holy Spirit the baptized who are continuing their journey of Christian initiation. By this sacrament the baptized are joined more perfectly to the Church, are strengthened, and are more strictly obliged to be witnesses to Christ by word and deed and to spread and defend the faith.

## Requirements for Confirmation

Canon 889,1. All and only the baptized who are not yet confirmed are capable of receiving confirmation.

2. Outside of danger of death, to receive confirmation licitly it is required, if one has the use of reason, that one be suitably instructed and properly disposed, and be able to renew one's baptismal promises.

## Preparation for Confirmation

Canon 890. The faithful are bound to receive this sacrament at the proper time. Parents, pastoral ministers, and especially pastors should see that the faithful are properly instructed to receive confirmation and that they do so at an opportune time.

## Age for Confirmation

Canon 891. The sacrament of confirmation should be conferred on the faithful around the age of discretion, unless the episcopal conference determines another age, or if there is danger of death, or if, in the judgment of the minister, a serious reason should support another age.

The traditional sequence for the reception of the sacraments of initiation is baptism first, confirmation second, and Eucharist third. Many theologians, liturgists, and others would like to see a return by local churches to the original practice of receiving confirmation before first Communion.

## Confirmation Sponsor

Canon 892. Insofar as possible, there should be a sponsor for the person to be confirmed. The sponsor's duty is to see that the one confirmed acts as a true witness to Christ and faithfully fulfills the duties inherent in this sacrament.

Canon 893,1. In order to be a sponsor, one must fulfill the conditions of c. 874.
2. It is expedient that one's baptismal godparent also serve as one's sponsor for confirmation.

Having the same sponsor for baptism and confirmation witnesses to the very close connection between these two sacraments of initiation.

# The Holy Eucharist

Canon 897. The Holy Eucharist is a most august sacrament in which Christ the Lord himself is contained, offered, and received, and by which the Church constantly lives and grows. The eucharistic sacrifice, the memorial of the Lord's death and resurrection, in which the sacrifice of the cross is perpetuated throughout the ages, is the summit and source of all worship and Christian life. It signifies and effects the unity of the people of God and builds up the body of Christ. The other sacraments and all the works of the ecclesiastical apostolate are closely connected with the Holy Eucharist and are directed toward it.

## Duties of the Faithful

Canon 898. The faithful should hold the Holy Eucharist in highest honor. They should take part actively in the celebration of the most august sacrifice, receive this sacrament very devoutly and frequently, and worship it with highest adoration. Pastoral ministers should explain the doctrine on this sacrament and zealously teach the faithful their duty.

## The Eucharistic Celebration

Canon 899,1. The Eucharistic celebration is the action of Christ himself and that of the Church. In the Eucharist Christ the Lord, through the ministry of the priest, offers to God the Father his very self substantially present under the form of bread and wine, and he gives himself as spiritual food to the faithful who are associated with his oblation.
2. In the eucharistic assembly the people of God are called together with the bishop or with the presiding priest under his authority acting in the person of Christ. All the faithful who take part in the Eucharist, whether clergy or laity, accompany him by participating in their own way according to the diversity of orders and liturgical functions.
3. The Eucharistic celebration is so arranged that all participants receive from it the many fruits for which Christ the Lord instituted the Eucharistic sacrifice.

### Observance of Proper Roles

Canon 907. In the Eucharistic celebration deacons and laypersons are not permitted to say the prayers, especially the Eucharistic prayer, or perform actions which are proper to the celebrating priest.

### Special Minister of Communion

Canon 910,2. The special minister of Communion is an acolyte or other member of the faithful who has been deputed in accord with c. 230,3.

C. 911,2 permits lay ministers of Communion to administer viaticum "in a case of necessity or with at least the presumed permission of the pastor, chaplain, or superior who must be notified afterwards."

## Reception of Communion

Canon 912. Any baptized person who is not prohibited by law may and must be admitted to Holy Communion.

## First Holy Communion

Canon 913,1. In order that the Holy Eucharist may be administered to children, it is required that they have sufficient knowledge and careful preparation so that they may perceive the mystery of Christ according to their capacity and be able to receive the body of the Lord with faith and devotion.
2. However, the Holy Eucharist may be administered to children in danger of death if they are able to distinguish the body of Christ from ordinary food and receive Communion reverently.
Canon 914. Parents, above all, those who take the place of parents, and pastors have the duty to see that children with the use of reason are duly prepared and are refreshed by this divine food as soon as possible, having previously made sacramental confession. It is also the duty of the pastor to be vigilant lest children come to the sacred banquet who do not have the use of reason or who he judges are not sufficiently disposed.

Concerning the issues of first confession before first Communion and the reception of the sacraments by the mentally handicapped, one should consult the policies of the diocese or national conference of bishops.

## Prohibition of Eucharist to Grave Sinners

Canon 915. Those who have been excommunicated or interdicted, after the infliction or declaration of the penalty, and others who obstinately persevere in manifest, serious sin are not to be admitted to Holy Communion.

Canon 916. One who is conscious of a serious sin may not celebrate Mass or receive the body of the Lord without previous sacramental confession unless there is a grave reason and there is no opportunity for confessing. In such a case the person should be mindful of the obligation to elicit an act of perfect contrition, which includes the intention of confessing as soon as possible.

## Communion Twice a Day

Canon 917. One who has already received the Holy Eucharist may receive it again on the same day only within the Eucharistic celebration at which he/she is participating, without prejudice to c. 921,2.

## Communion Outside Mass

Canon 918. It is highly recommended that the faithful receive Holy Communion in the eucharistic celebration itself. However, for a just cause it may be administered outside of Mass to those who request it, observing the liturgical rites.

## Eucharistic Fast

Canon 919,1. One who is to receive the Holy Eucharist should abstain from all food and drink, except for water and medicine, for at least one hour before Holy Communion.

## Some Exceptions to Fast

Canon 919,3. Those who are advanced in age or who suffer from some infirmity and those who care for

them may receive the Holy Eucharist even if they
have taken something within the previous hour.

"Those who care" for the sick and aged can be understood to
include family members and visitors who provide spiritual and
emotional support, not just those who are providing physical
care.

## Easter Duty

Canon 920,1. All the faithful, once they have been
admitted to the Holy Eucharist, are obliged to receive
Holy Communion at least once a year.
2. This precept must be fulfilled during Easter time
unless for a just reason it is fulfilled at some other
time during the year.

In the United States the Easter duty may be fulfilled within
the period from the first Sunday of Lent through Trinity
Sunday.

## Viaticum

Canon 921,1. The faithful who are in danger of
death for any reason at all should be refreshed by
Holy Communion in the form of viaticum.
2. Even if they have received Holy Communion that
same day, it is nevertheless highly recommended
that those who are near a dangerous crisis should
receive again.
3. While the danger of death persists, it is recommended that Holy Communion be administered
often but on separate days.
Canon 922. Holy viaticum for the sick should not be
delayed too long. Those in pastoral work should be
zealously vigilant that the sick receive it while fully
conscious.

Viaticum is the last sacrament—not the anointing of the sick—unless the person is unable to receive Communion. Viaticum is Holy Communion given to those who are at the hour of death or who are in danger of dying. It is the spiritual food which is intended to give dying persons the strength and comfort needed to travel the last stage of their earthly journey and refresh them for the next life.

## Eucharist in Other Rites

Canon 923. The faithful are able to participate in the Eucharistic sacrifice and receive Holy Communion in any Catholic rite, c. 844 remaining in effect.

## Communion under One or Both Kinds

Canon 925. Holy Communion may be given under the form of bread alone or, according to the norm of the liturgical laws, under both kinds; but in case of need, it may even be given under the form of wine alone.

It is preferable by reason of its symbolic value to receive Communion under both kinds because this is the way Christ gave it at the Last Supper. Communion may be received in the form of wine alone by those who for medical reasons are unable to receive it in the form of bread.

## Latin Masses

Canon 928. The Eucharist may be celebrated in Latin or some other language provided the liturgical texts have been legitimately approved.

## Personal Possession of the Eucharist

> Canon 935. No one may keep the Holy Eucharist in one's possession or take it on a trip, except in urgent pastoral necessity and observing the prescriptions of the diocesan bishop.

This prohibition does not refer to ministers of the Eucharist when they have lawful possession of the Eucharist for pastoral need, such as when they bring Communion to the sick.

## Prayer Before the Blessed Sacrament

> Canon 937. Unless a serious reason prevents it, a church in which the Holy Eucharist is reserved should be open to the faithful for at least some hours each day so that they may be free to pray before the Blessed Sacrament.

## Special Ministers of Exposition

> Canon 943. The minister of exposition and benediction of the holy sacrament of the Eucharist is a priest or deacon. In special circumstances the exposition and reposition only, but not the benediction, may be done by an acolyte, a special minister of Holy Communion, or some other person deputed by the local ordinary, observing the prescriptions of the diocesan bishop.

## Offerings for the Celebration of Mass

> Canon 946. The faithful who give an offering that Mass be applied for their intention contribute to the good of the Church and participate in the Church's concern for the support of its ministers and works.

A *Mass offering* is the term in the revised Code for what was commonly called a Mass "stipend." The term "stipend" was used in the ancient Roman empire for the wage paid to soldiers. The Church prefers the word "offering" because it better signifies that the money given for the application of Mass according to a particular intention is not payment for services rendered, but is a freewill donation to the Church to help support its ministers and ministries. Although the donation is freely made, a set amount for the offering is usually established for a region. This is desirable not only because a chief purpose of the Mass offering system is the support of the Church, but also to avoid abuses and to ensure uniformity of practice.

# Penance

Canon 959. In the sacrament of penance the faithful confess their sins to a legitimate minister, are sorry for them, and resolve to reform. Through the absolution imparted by this minister they obtain from God pardon for their sins committed after baptism, and they are reconciled with the Church which they have wounded by sinning.

## Individual Confession

Canon 960. Individual and integral confession and absolution constitute the only ordinary way by which the faithful who are conscious of serious sin are reconciled with God and the Church. Only physical or moral impossibility excuses from this kind of confession, in which case there also may be reconciliation in other ways.

*General Absolution*

> Canon 962,1. That the faithful may receive a valid absolution given to many at the same time it is required not only that they be properly disposed but likewise have the intention in due time to confess individually their serious sins which at present they are unable to so confess.
>
> Canon 963. One whose serious sins are remitted by a general absolution should go to individual confession as soon as there is the opportunity. This should be done before receiving another general absolution, unless a just cause intervenes. The obligation of c. 989 remains effective.

According to c. 961, general absolution is intended to be used only in situations of necessity such as on occasions when there are too many penitents to be handled by the number of confessors available. Those who have serious sins and receive a general absolution must have the intention of confessing these sins individually as soon as they have the opportunity. Meanwhile, they are absolved fully and may receive the sacraments. Venial sins absolved by a general absolution do not need to be confessed subsequently.

*The Penance*

> Canon 981. The confessor should impose salutary and appropriate penances according to the kind and number of sins, keeping in mind the penitent's condition. The penitent is bound by obligation to fulfill the penance personally.

*False Denunciation of a Confessor*

> Canon 982. If anyone confesses that he/she had falsely denounced an innocent confessor of the crime

of solicitation to sin against the Sixth Commandment, that person should not be absolved unless he/she first formally retracts the false denunciation and is prepared to make amends for damages, if there are any.

## Seal of Confession

Canon 983,1. The sacramental seal is inviolable. Therefore it is sinful for the confessor to betray the penitent either by words or by any other means for any reason whatsoever.
2. Also bound to the observance of secrecy are the interpreter, if there is one, and all others who have gained knowledge in any way of a sinner's confession.
Canon 984,1. The confessor is totally prohibited from using knowledge acquired in confession to the detriment of the penitent, even when there is no danger of revelation.

## The Penitent

Canon 987. In order that the faithful might receive the healing remedy of the sacrament of penance, they must be so disposed that they are converted to God by repudiating the sins which they committed and having the intention to reform their lives.

## Mortal and Venial Sins

Canon 988,1. The faithful are bound by obligation to confess the kind and number of all serious sins committed after baptism which are not yet directly remitted by the keys of the Church and admitted in individual confession. They are to confess those serious sins of which they are conscious after a diligent examination of conscience.

2. It is recommended that the faithful also confess their venial sins.

## Precept to Confess Annually

Canon 989. All the faithful, after they have reached the age of discretion, are bound to confess faithfully their serious sins at least once a year.

## Interpreter in Confession

Canon 990. No one is prohibited from confessing through an interpreter provided all abuses and scandals are avoided and c. 983,2 is observed.

## Confession in Other Rites

Canon 991. All the faithful are at liberty to confess their sins to a legitimately approved confessor of their own choice, even to one of another rite.

## Indulgences

Canon 992. An indulgence is the remission before God of the temporal punishment for sins already forgiven. Indulgences are obtained by the faithful who are suitably disposed and who meet certain specified conditions. Indulgences are derived through means of the Church which authoritatively dispenses and applies the treasury of reparations made by Christ and the saints.

## Partial and Plenary Indulgences

Canon 993. An indulgence is partial or plenary insofar as it partly or totally frees one from the temporal punishment for sins.

Canon 994. Any member of the faithful may personally gain partial or plenary indulgences or apply them to the dead by way of intercessory prayer.

## Capability to Gain Indulgences

Canon 996,1. Anyone is capable of gaining indulgences who is baptized, not excommunicated, and in the state of grace at least at the end of the prescribed works.

2. But to actually obtain indulgences the capable person must have at least the intention to acquire them and fulfill the works connected with them within the stated time and in the required manner, in accord with the tenor of the concession.

# Anointing of the Sick

Canon 998. Through the anointing of the sick the Church commends to the suffering and glorified Lord the faithful who are seriously ill that he may comfort them and heal them. The sacrament is conferred by anointing them with oil and saying the words prescribed in the liturgical books.

## Those Who May Be Anointed

Canon 1004,1. The anointing of the sick may be administered to the faithful who have the use of reason and begin to fall into danger as a result of illness or old age.

2. This sacrament may be repeated if the sick person has become better and again falls into a serious illness or, if during the same illness, a more serious crisis develops.

Canon 1005. If there is doubt whether the sick person has the use of reason, is seriously ill, or is dead, the sacrament may be administered.

Canon 1006. The sacrament may be conferred on the sick who, when they were in control of their faculties, had at least implicitly asked for it.

Canon 1007. The anointing of the sick should not be conferred on those who obstinately remain in manifest, serious sin.

# Orders

Canon 1008. By divine institution some of the faithful are made ordained ministers through the sacrament of orders by which they are marked with an indelible character. They are consecrated and commissioned to shepherd the people of God, each according to his grade, fulfilling in the person of Christ the head the functions of teaching, sanctifying, and governing.

The grades of orders are those of deacon, priest, and bishop.

## Ordinations

Canon 1011,2. The clergy and other members of the faithful are to be invited to an ordination so that a very large assembly may participate in the celebration.

## Impediments to Ordination

Canon 1043. The faithful are obliged to reveal to the ordinary or pastor before the ordination any impediments to holy orders which they may know.

The impediments to holy orders are treated in cc. 1040–1049.

# Marriage

The Church's marriage law is quite complex. The canons selected here are those generally more readily understood without lengthy explanation and more directly useful to a general audience than many of the other canons from this section of the Code.

## *The Matrimonial Covenant*

> Canon 1055,1. The matrimonial covenant among the baptized was raised by Christ the Lord to the dignity of a sacrament. By it a man and woman establish among themselves a total community of life which by its very nature is ordained for the good of the spouses and the procreation and education of children.
> 2. Therefore any valid contract of marriage between the baptized is by that very fact a sacrament.

## *Essential Properties of Marriage*

> Canon 1056. The essential properties of marriage are unity and indissolubility which in Christian marriage obtain a particular firmness by reason of its sacramentality.

Unity means that marriage is between one man and one woman; it is monogamous and exclusive. Indissolubility means that the marriage bond is permanent until death and cannot be broken by any human authority. The Church does not recognize civil divorce.

## *Marital Consent*

> Canon 1057,1. Marriage is made by the consent of the parties legitimately manifested between persons

capable by law. No human power is able to supply
consent for the parties.
2. Marital consent is an act of the will by which a
man and a woman through an irrevocable covenant
mutually hand over and accept each other in order
to establish matrimony.

The free and mature consent of capable persons makes a
marriage come to be. No one else can give this consent except
the man and woman who are marrying. If this consent is lacking or is legally defective in some way, there is no marriage
even if it were performed before the Church's minister and two
witnesses. Most marital annulments are granted on some
grounds related to defective consent. Consent is treated further
in cc. 1095–1107.

## Preparation for Marriage

Canon 1065,1. Before they are allowed to marry,
Catholics who have not yet received the sacrament
of confirmation should receive it if it can be done
without serious inconvenience.
2. In order to receive the sacrament of marriage
fruitfully, the engaged couple is earnestly encour-
aged to go to the sacraments of penance and Holy
Eucharist.

Other requirements for marriage preparation are given in
cc. 1063–1068 and the particular law of dioceses and episcopal
conferences.

## Impediments to Marriage

Canon 1069. Before the celebration of a marriage,
all the faithful who know of any impediments are
bound to reveal them to the pastor or local ordinary.

An impediment is some fact or condition which according to canon law renders a person incapable of contracting marriage validly. Cc. 1083–1094 establish the impediments of non-age, impotence, prior bond, disparity of cult, holy orders, public perpetual vow of chastity in a religious institute, abduction, crime, consanguinity, affinity, public honesty, and legal relationship. Two of these impediments are of divine law and therefore are not dispensable: prior bond, which is the bond of a previous marriage, that is, a former spouse who is still living; and impotence which is antecedent to marriage and perpetual. Dispensations are never granted for the impediment of consanguinity in the direct line (for a direct ancestor to marry a direct descendant, such as for a father to marry his daughter), or in the second degree collateral (for a brother to marry his sister). First cousins need a dispensation to marry; second cousins do not. Dispensations are readily granted for disparity of cult, that is, a marriage of a Catholic with a non-baptized person.

## Age for Marriage

> Canon 1072. Pastoral ministers should see to it that young people are diverted from marrying before the age which is customary in the region.

A boy under 16 or a girl under 14 may not marry validly. The episcopal conference of a nation may establish a higher age for licit marriage. Except in necessity, no minister without the permission of the local ordinary may perform the marriage ceremony of a person under 18 whose parents are opposed to it.

## Officiants at Weddings

> Canon 1112,1. The diocesan bishop may delegate laypersons to assist at weddings when priests and

deacons are lacking, provided the episcopal conference had previously voted to permit this and permission was obtained from the Apostolic See.
2. A worthy layperson should be chosen who is capable of handling the pre-marital instructions and who
can correctly perform the matrimonial rites.

Ordinarily the marriage ceremony of a Catholic must be
conducted by a priest or deacon who has the faculty to ask for
the couple's marital consent and to receive it in the name of the
Church. The minister who does this is said to *assist* at marriage. Also required is the presence of two witnesses, typically
the maid of honor and the best man. The assisting presence of
the Church's minister and the presence of the two witnesses
constitute the form of marriage, also called the canonical form.
This canonical form is necessary for the valid marriage of any
Catholic in ordinary circumstances. A chief reason for the requirement of the canonical form is to ensure that marriages
are publicly recognized and recorded. However, since it is *consent* between the parties that makes the marriage and not the
church ceremony, there are some exceptions to the canonical
form permitted by the law as follows:

1) *Laypersons assisting at marriages.* The above canon provides for those areas where there are not sufficient clergy to
handle all the marriages, such as in mission lands.

2) *Dispensations from canonical form* may be given in
mixed marriages according to the norm of c. 1127,2,3. For
example, a Protestant woman wishes to marry a Catholic
man in her church before the Protestant minister. For the
validity of this marriage the Catholic must receive a dispensation from canonical form.

3) *Catholic/Orthodox marriages.* For a Catholic to marry a
member of a non-Catholic eastern church before the minister of that church, a dispensation from canonical form is not
required for the *validity* of the marriage (c. 1127,1). This

exception recognizes the privileged status of the eastern churches in the eyes of the Catholic Church.

4) *In danger of death,* when an official minister of the Church cannot be reached, a couple may marry before witnesses alone (c. 1116,1,n.1).

5) *In the absence of an official minister* of the Church—as long as it is prudently foreseen that this absence will continue for a month or more—a couple may marry before witnesses alone. For example, a couple who live in a remote area of the world wish to marry, but they believe that the priest or other minister will not be present for at least a month (c. 1116,1,n.2).

6) *Common error,* such as when a priest or deacon does not have the faculty to assist at marriage but does so anyway and the people present mistakenly believe that he does have the faculty. In such a case *the Church supplies* the faculty in order that the marriage is not invalidated by reason of a mere legal technicality (c. 144). C. 144 also includes the case of positive and probable doubt of law or of fact.

## Place of Marriage

Canon 1115. Marriages should be celebrated in the parish where either of the contracting parties has a domicile or quasi-domicile or a month's residence. If it is a question of the marriage of wanderers, it takes place in the parish where the wanderers are actually staying. With permission of the proper ordinary or proper pastor, it may be celebrated elsewhere.

Canon 1118,1. A marriage between Catholics or between a Catholic party and a baptized non-Catholic party is celebrated in a parish church. It may be celebrated in another church or oratory with the permission of the local ordinary or pastor.

2. The local ordinary can also permit a marriage to be celebrated in some other suitable place.

3. A marriage between a Catholic party and a non-baptized party may be celebrated in church or in some other suitable place.

## Mixed Marriages

Canon 1124. A mixed marriage is prohibited without the express permission of the competent authority. A mixed marriage is a marriage between two baptized persons, one who was baptized in the Catholic Church or was received into it after baptism and who has not left it by a formal act, and the other who belongs to a church or ecclesial community which does not have full communion with the Catholic Church.

In brief, a mixed marriage is one between a Catholic and a baptized non-Catholic. Such marriages require the *permission* of the local ordinary, but not for validity as is the case for a marriage between a Catholic and a non-baptized person which requires a *dispensation*.

## The Promises in a Mixed Marriage

Canon 1125. The local ordinary is able to grant permission for a mixed marriage if there is a just and reasonable cause. He should not grant it unless the following conditions are fulfilled:
1) The Catholic party should declare that he/she is prepared to remove dangers of falling away from the faith and should make a sincere promise to do all in his/her power to have all the children baptized and brought up in the Catholic Church.
2) The other party should be informed at a suitable time of the Catholic party's promises so that it is clear that the non-Catholic is truly conscious

of the promise and obligation of the Catholic party.

3) Both parties should be instructed on the ends and essential properties of marriage which are not to be excluded by either spouse.

The ends and essential properties of marriage are given in cc. 1055–1056. The provisions of this canon must also be observed for marriages between a Catholic and a non-baptized person.

## Secret Celebration of Marriage

Canon 1130. For a serious and urgent cause the local ordinary may permit a marriage to be celebrated in secret.

Further norms on secret marriages are given in cc. 1131–1133.

## The Effects of Marriage

Canon 1134. From a valid marriage there arise between the spouses a bond which by its nature is perpetual and exclusive. Moreover, in Christian marriage the spouses by a special sacrament are strengthened and, as it were, are consecrated for the duties and dignity of their marital state.

## Equality of Spouses

Canon 1135. Both spouses have the equal duty and right to those things which pertain to the community of conjugal life.

## Duty and Right of Parents

> Canon 1136. Parents have a most serious duty and the primary right to do all in their power to provide for their children's physical, social, cultural, moral, and religious upbringing.

## Legitimate and Illegitimate Children

> Canon 1137. Children are legitimate if they are conceived or born from a valid or putative marriage.

A putative marriage is one that is celebrated in good faith by at least one party, that is, at least one spouse thought he/she was marrying validly. Hence, when one obtains an annulment of marriage the legitimacy of the children is not affected because at the time when the marriage was celebrated at least one of the spouses very likely believed he/she was marrying validly. Further norms on legitimacy of children are found in cc. 1138–1140.

## Annulment and Dissolution

> Canon 1141. A ratified and consummated marriage cannot be dissolved by any human power or by any cause other than death.

A ratified marriage is a valid marriage between two baptized persons. It is also called a *sacramental* marriage. When such a marriage is consummated it is considered indissoluble—no divorce and remarriage is permitted. The basis for this law lies in Christ's teaching on divorce in the gospels, as reflected in the words: "What God has joined together, let no one put asunder." For this reason the Church requires that a person who had previously attempted marriage must receive an *annulment* of that marriage before he/she can marry validly in the Church. An annulment is an official declaration by the Church of the invalidity of a marriage. It implies that the Church does not consider the marriage in question to have been valid from the beginning on the basis of some canonical reason, such as defective consent.

A *dissolution* of marriage is more like a "Church divorce" because it does not question the validity of the marriage. In accord with c. 1142, the pope can grant a dissolution for marriages that are not consummated. The law also permits the dissolution of non-sacramental marriages in accord with the norm of cc. 1143–1150 and other established procedures.

## Separation and Divorce

> Canon 1151. Spouses have the duty and right to observe conjugal life unless a legitimate reason excuses them.

Legitimate reasons for which an innocent spouse may petition for an ecclesiastical separation are: (1) adultery of one spouse; (2) serious bodily or spiritual danger to a spouse or the children which is caused by the other spouse; (3) difficulty in enduring common life due to the conduct of one spouse. The norms for ecclesiastical separation are found in cc. 1152–1155. In many countries, including the United States, ecclesiastical separations are rare. In such places Catholics usually effect a separation on their own or by civil divorce. Such separated or divorced persons are able to remain practicing Catholics and receive the sacraments provided they do not remarry outside the Church. Those who have remarried outside the Church should see a priest or someone knowledgeable in canon law to determine if there is a possibility for an annulment or some other means of returning to the sacraments.

# Part II
# Other Acts of Divine Worship

## Sacramentals

> Canon 1166. Sacramentals are sacred signs, some-
> what akin to sacraments. These sacred signs signify
> their effects, especially spiritual ones, which are ob-
> tained by the intercession of the Church.

## Ministers of Sacramentals

> Canon 1168. The minister of sacramentals is a cler-
> ic who has the necessary power. In accordance with
> the liturgical books and in the judgment of the local
> ordinary, certain sacramentals may also be admin-
> istered by qualified laypersons.

## The Liturgy of the Hours

> Canon 1174,2. According to circumstances, lay
> members of the faithful should be earnestly invited
> to participate in the liturgy of the hours inasmuch
> as it is an action of the Church.

The liturgy of the hours, also called the Divine Office, is part
of the Church's official liturgical prayer. The most important
hours are Morning Prayer (Lauds) and Evening Prayer
(Vespers).

## Burial and Cremation

> Canon 1176,3. The Church earnestly recommends
> that the pious custom of burying the bodies of the
> dead be observed. However, cremation is not prohib-

ited unless it is chosen for reasons contrary to Christian doctrine.

## Place of Funeral Rites

Canon 1177,1. Generally the funeral rites of any deceased member of the faithful must be celebrated in one's own parish church.

2. However, each of the faithful is allowed to choose another church for the funeral with the consent of the rector of that church. One's pastor should be notified of this arrangement. One may personally choose the other church, or it may be done by the person who is in charge of the funeral arrangements.

3. If death occurs outside one's parish and the body was not returned to it, and another church was not legitimately chosen for the funeral, the funeral rites should be celebrated in the parish church within whose boundaries the death occurred, unless particular law has specified another church.

## Cemeteries

Canon 1180,1. If the parish has its own cemetery, the faithful departed are to be buried in it unless another cemetery was legitimately chosen by the deceased or by those who have charge of the burial.

2. However, all may choose their own cemetery, unless they are prohibited by law.

## Those Granted Church Funerals

Canon 1183,1. Catechumens are equated with the faithful in matters pertaining to funeral rites.

2. The local ordinary can permit ecclesiastical fu-

neral rites for children who died before baptism if their parents had intended to have them baptized.

3. In the prudent judgment of the local ordinary, ecclesiastical funeral rites can be granted to baptized persons belonging to some non-Catholic church or ecclesial community, provided they are unable to have their own minister. This cannot be done if it is against their wishes.

## Those Denied Church Funerals

Canon 1184,1. Unless before death there was some indication of repentance, ecclesiastical funeral rites are denied to:

    1) notorious apostates, heretics, and schismatics;

    2) those who have chosen the cremation of their bodies for reasons contrary to the Christian faith;

    3) other manifest sinners for whom ecclesiastical funeral rites cannot be conducted without public scandal to the faithful.

2. If any doubt occurs in this matter, one should consult the local ordinary whose decision is to be followed.

Canon 1185. Any funeral Mass whatsoever is also to be denied to someone who is excluded from ecclesiastical funeral rites.

## The Cult of Mary and Other Saints

Canon 1186. To foster the sanctification of the people of God, the Church commends for the faithful's special and filial veneration the blessed Mary ever virgin, Mother of God, whom Christ made the Mother of all people. The Church also promotes the true and authentic cult of the other saints who edify the faithful by their example and who sustain them by their intercession.

Canon 1187. Only those servants of God may be venerated in public worship who are recorded by the authority of the Church in the register of saints and blesseds.

## *Sacred Images*

Canon 1188. The practice of displaying sacred images in churches for the veneration of the faithful should continue. However, they should be exhibited in moderate numbers and in suitable fashion lest they cause wonderment among the Christian people or occasion a somewhat less correct devotion.

## *Relics*

Canon 1190,1. It is sinful to sell sacred relics.

## *Vows and Oaths*

Canon 1191,1. A vow is a deliberate and free promise made to God concerning a possible and better good. The virtue of religion requires that it must be fulfilled.
Canon 1199,1. An oath is the invocation of the divine name in witness to the truth. It is taken only in truth, judgment, or justice.

# *Part III*
# *Sacred Places and Sacred Times*

## Sacred Places

Canon 1205. Sacred places are those places which are deputed for divine worship or the burial of the faithful. Sacred places are deputed by a dedication or blessing as prescribed in the liturgical books.

## Churches

Canon 1214. By the word "church" is understood a sacred building intended for divine worship to which the faithful have a right to go for divine worship, especially when it is carried out publicly.

## Free Admittance to Churches

Canon 1221. Entrance to a church at the time of sacred celebrations should be free and gratuitous.

## Oratories

Canon 1223. By the word "oratory" is understood a place for divine worship established with the permission of the ordinary for the good of some community or group of the faithful who assemble there. Other members of the faithful may also go there with the permission of the competent superior.

A common example of an oratory is the place of worship connected with a religious house. The major distinction between a church and an oratory is that the faithful have a *right* to go to a church whereas they may go to an oratory with permission of the competent superior.

## Private Chapels

Canon 1226. By the term "private chapel" is understood a place established with the permission of the local ordinary for divine worship for the good of one or more physical persons.

The law allows bishops to establish private chapels for themselves. Other private chapels may be established only with the permission of the local ordinary.

## Shrines

> Canon 1230. A "shrine" is a church or other sacred place which the faithful, with the approval of the local ordinary, regularly visit for some special reason of devotion.

## Altars

> Canon 1235,1. An altar is a table on which the Eucharistic sacrifice is celebrated. It is *fixed* if it is so constructed that it is secured to the floor and cannot be moved. It is *moveable* if it can be transferred.
> 2. It is fitting to have a fixed altar in every church. In other places established for sacred celebrations the altar may be fixed or moveable.

## Cemeteries

> Canon 1241,1. Parishes and religious institutes may have their own cemetery.
> 2. Also other juridic persons or families may have a particular cemetery or burial place to be blessed according to the judgment of the local ordinary.

# Sacred Times

## Sundays and Holy Days

> Canon 1246,1. Sunday, the day on which the paschal mystery is celebrated, is by apostolic tradition to be

observed in the whole Church as the primordial feast day of obligation. The other holy days of obligation are: Christmas, Epiphany, Ascension, Corpus Christi, Mary Mother of God, Immaculate Conception, Assumption, St. Joseph, Sts. Peter and Paul, and All Saints.

2. However, the episcopal conference, with the previous approval of the Apostolic See, may abolish the obligation connected to some holy days or transfer their celebration to Sunday.

## Feast Day Obligations

Canon 1247. On Sundays and holy days of obligation the faithful are bound to participate at Mass. Moreover, they should abstain from work and business which might impede the worship to be rendered to God, or the joy proper to the Lord's day, or due relaxation of mind and body.

## Anticipated Evening Masses

Canon 1248,1. The precept to participate at Mass is satisfied by anyone who attends Mass wherever it is celebrated in a Catholic rite on the day of obligation itself or in the evening of the preceding day.

## Substitutions for Mass Attendance

Canon 1248,2. If an ordained minister is unavailable or there is some other serious reason which makes it impossible to participate in the Eucharistic celebration, it is highly recommended that the faithful take part in the liturgy of the Word if it is celebrated in a parish church or other sacred place in accordance with the prescriptions of the diocesan bishop. The faithful may also have prayers for a suitable time either personally, as a family, or in groups of families if opportune.

In particular cases the pastor may dispense from the obligations of Sundays and holy days for a just reason. He may also substitute other pious acts in place of the obligations.

## Days of Penance

Canon 1249. All the faithful, in their own way, are bound by divine law to do penance. But in order that all might be joined together in some common observance of penance, penitential days are prescribed. On these days the faithful pray in a special way; they perform works of piety and charity; and they mortify themselves by fulfilling their proper duties more faithfully, and especially by observing fast and abstinence in accord with the canons which follow.

## Fridays and Lent

Canon 1250. The penitential days and times in the universal Church are Fridays and the season of Lent.

## Days of Fast and Abstinence

Canon 1251. Unless a solemnity falls on that day, every Friday is to be observed as a day of abstinence from meat or from some other food in accord with the prescriptions of the episcopal conference. Fast and abstinence are to be observed on Ash Wednesday and Good Friday.

## Age for Fast and Abstinence

> Canon 1252. Those who are 14 and older are bound by the law of abstinence. Bound to fast are all those adults from age 18 to the beginning of their 60th year. Moreover, pastoral ministers and parents should see to it that minors who are not bound to the law of fast and abstinence are instilled with a genuine sense of penance.

## Substitutions for Fast and Abstinence

> Canon 1253. The episcopal conference can determine more exactly the observance of fast and abstinence and in their place may totally or partially substitute other forms of penance, especially works of charity and exercises of piety.

In particular cases the pastor may dispense from the obligations of fast and abstinence for a just reason. He may also substitute other pious acts in place of these obligations.

# Book V
# The Temporal Goods of the Church

In order to fulfill its divine mission the Church necessarily must have temporal goods. Without adequate properties and financial resources the Church would be hindered in carrying out its various charitable, educational, and ministerial endeavors. Book V establishes general rules for the administration of temporal goods throughout the universal Church. It is the shortest book of the Code with only 57 canons. These canons are mainly of interest to Church administrators and financial officers, and for that reason very few of them are given here.

*The Acquisition of Goods*

> Canon 1260. The Church has an inherent right to ask the faithful for the things necessary for its proper ends.

## Support of the Church

> Canon 1261,1. The faithful are at liberty to confer temporal goods on behalf of the Church.
> 2. The diocesan bishop in a fitting way must educate and exhort the faithful about the obligation which is stated in c. 222,1.

C. 222,1 is the obligation of the faithful to support the Church and its works.

> Canon 1262. The faithful should provide support to the Church by giving the assistance requested, and in accord with the norms of the episcopal conference.

## Unauthorized Collections Prohibited

> Canon 1265,1. Without prejudice to the right of mendicant religious, all private persons, whether physical or juridic, are prohibited from collecting contributions for any pious or ecclesiastical institution or purpose without the written permission of their own ordinary and the local ordinary.

## The Administration of Goods

> Canon 1282. All persons, clergy and laity, who by any lawful title have a part in the administration of ecclesiastical goods, are bound to fulfill their duties in the name of the Church according to the norm of law.

The laws governing the administration of Church goods are found principally in Book V, especially cc. 1273–1289. Members of parish or diocesan finance councils are among those clergy and laity who may have a particular interest in these canons.

## Bequests to the Church

> Canon 1299,1. Those who by natural or canon law are free to dispose of their goods may leave them to pious causes. This may be done either by an act of the living or by an act which is effective at death.

# Book VI
# Sanctions in the Church

Since the Church is a human society as well as the Spirit-filled people of God, it must possess the means to punish members who commit serious infractions against the divine law or Church discipline. By specifying certain grave offenses as crimes subject to punishment, the Church hopes to deter the commission of such crimes against God and religion, and to lead sinners to repentance by making them aware of the gravity of their offense. The penal law of the universal Church is given in Book VI of the Code. It reflects a substantial revision and simplification of the former discipline. There were 220 canons on penal law in the 1917 Code, and there are only 89 in the 1983 Code. Nevertheless, penal law remains a rather complex area for the non-expert and for the most part is beyond the purview of this work.

## The Censure of Excommunication

Canon 1331,1. The excommunicate is prohibited from:

> 1) having any ministerial participation in the celebration of the Eucharistic Sacrifice or in any other ceremonies of worship;
> 2) celebrating the sacraments or sacramentals or receiving the sacraments;
> 3) serving in any ecclesiastical offices, ministries, or functions, or placing acts of governance.

The penalty of *automatic excommunication reserved to the Apostolic See* is incurred by the commission of any of the following crimes: violation of the consecrated bread or wine (c. 1367); a physical attack on the pope (c. 1370,1); absolution of an accomplice in a sin against the Sixth Commandment (c. 1378); unauthorized consecration of a bishop (c. 1382); direct violation by a confessor of the seal of confession (c. 1388). The non-reserved automatic excommunications are those incurred for the crimes of apostasy, heresy, or schism (c. 1364,1); and for procuring an abortion (c. 1398). The reservation of penalties to the Apostolic See means that the Apostolic See is the competent authority to remove the penalty. Other penalties are removed in accordance with the provisions of cc. 1354–1363.

No one can incur an ecclesiastical penalty unless the crime has been perfectly committed according to the strict letter of the law. There are many circumstances which mitigate the severity of penalties or excuse from them altogether. These circumstances are treated chiefly in cc. 1321–1330. Automatic penalties, such as the automatic excommunication for the crime of abortion, would not be incurred under such circumstances as when the person: is under eighteen; acts out of serious fear, even if only relatively serious; acts through necessity or serious disadvantage; is unaware without any fault of his/her own that a penalty was attached to the law. Such factors must be carefully weighed, particularly by one's confessor, before determining whether an automatic penalty truly has been incurred.

## The Censure of Interdict

> Canon 1332. Those who are interdicted are bound by the prohibitions of c. 1331,1,nn.1 and 2; but if the interdict has been imposed or declared, the prescription of c. 1331,2,n.1 must be observed.

It is extremely rare in many countries for a Church authority to impose excommunication, interdict, or other penalties on laypersons, or to declare that a penalty has been incurred automatically. Hence, *imposed* or *declared* censures are of little concern here in comparison to automatic censures.

The interdicted are prohibited from: (1) having any ministerial participation in the celebration of the Eucharistic Sacrifice or in any other ceremonies of worship; and (2) celebrating the sacraments or sacramentals or receiving the sacraments. An automatic interdict is incurred by the commission of the following crimes: physical attack on a bishop (1370,2); pretended celebration of the Eucharist by a non-priest (c. 1378,2,n.1); attempt to impart sacramental absolution or hear confessions by one who cannot do so validly (c. 1378,2,n.2); false accusation of the crime of solicitation in the confessional (c. 1390,1); attempted marriage by a religious in perpetual vows (c. 1394,2). The commission of any of these same crimes by a cleric results in *suspension* which has additional penal effects.

Not all penalties are as severe as the censures of excommunication, interdict, and suspension. For many crimes the Code states that a "just penalty" may be imposed, which means that the severity of the penalty administered by the judge or ordinary is in accord with the gravity and circumstances of the crime. The following are examples of some crimes listed in the Code for which various penalties may be imposed:

—prohibited participation in the rites of another faith (c. 1365);

—parents, or those who take the place of parents, who willingly have their children baptized or educated in a non-Catholic religion (c. 1366);

—perjury before an ecclesiastical authority (c. 1368);

—abusing the Church or religious values in a public forum or in the media (c. 1369);

—use of physical force against a cleric or religious out of contempt for the Church (c. 1370,3);

—teaching a doctrine condemned by a pope or an ecumenical council (c. 1371,n.1);

—direct violation of the seal of confession by an interpreter or someone else who has knowledge of another's confession (c. 1388,2);

—calumnious denunciation to an ecclesiastical superior of an offense, or injury to the good reputation of another (c. 1390,2);

—falsification of public Church documents (c. 1391).

# Book VII
# Procedures

Disputes among people inevitably arise at times in every human society, and it is therefore necessary to have reliable and equitable structures and procedures for resolving such disputes. The final book of the Code establishes judicial and administrative procedures for handling disputes within the Church. With 353 canons it is a long, detailed, and complex book mostly of interest to officials of Church courts, or tribunals. Despite the technical nature of Book VII, there are some canons which may be of interest to the non-specialist. Above all, it should be noted that all the offices and functions in Church tribunals may be held by lay men and women except for the offices of vicar judicial and adjutant vicar judicial (officialis and vice-officialis) who must be priests. The vicar judicial is the head judge, the one who is in charge of running the tribunal; the adjutant vicar judicial is his assistant.

## Judges

> Canon 1421,1. The bishop should appoint for his diocese diocesan judges who are clerics.
> 2. The episcopal conference may permit laypersons to be judges; in case of need a lay judge may be one of the members of a collegiate tribunal.
> 3. Judges should be of irreproachable reputation and have the doctorate or licentiate in canon law.

Ordinarily marriage cases are tried by a collegiate tribunal, that is, a college or group of three judges. One of these judges may be a lay man or woman who has the proper qualifications.

## Assessors

> Canon 1424. In any trial a single judge may take two assessors as consultors who may be either clergy or laity of good reputation.

By exception, a case may be heard in the first instance by a single clerical judge according to the provisions of c. 1425,4. Such a judge should make use of the services of an assessor and auditor, if possible. Unlike judges, assessors and auditors are not required to have academic degrees in canon law.

## Auditors

> Canon 1428,1. A judge or president of a collegiate tribunal may appoint an auditor to carry out the instruction of a case. He/she is selected from among the tribunal's judges or from the persons approved by the bishop for this task.
> 2. The bishop may appoint to the office of auditor either clerics or laypersons who demonstrate good morals, prudence, and learning.

3. The task of the auditor, according to the mandate of the judge, is only to collect the proofs and give them to the judge. Nevertheless, unless the mandate of the judge states otherwise, auditors may at times decide which proofs are to be collected and how they are to be collected if such questions arise while they are fulfilling their duties.

One of the main tasks in marriage annulment cases is the gathering of proofs to demonstrate the validity or invalidity of the marriage. Some common sources of proofs are documentary evidence and the testimony of witnesses. Trained lay auditors can be of great assistance to Church tribunals in collecting such proofs.

## Promotor of Justice and Defender of the Bond

Canon 1435. The bishop should appoint a promotor of justice and a defender of the bond. They may be clergy or laity of good reputation with the licentiate or doctorate in canon law and recognized for their prudence and zeal for justice.

The task of the promotor of justice is to provide for the public good of the Church in contentious cases, somewhat akin to a prosecuting attorney in civil society. The defender of the bond is required for all marriage cases to defend the bond of marriage against those who are contending that it is null. The defender is akin to a defense attorney for the Church which desires to uphold the validity of its sacraments.

## Notary

Canon 1437,1. A notary must be present for all proceedings. Any acts are null if they are not signed by the notary.

The notary in Church courts functions like civil notaries by officially witnessing and signing the acts of the case.

## Avoidance of Litigation

> Canon 1446,1. All the faithful, but especially bishops, should zealously strive, without prejudice to justice, to avoid conflicts among the people of God as much as possible, and to settle them peacefully as soon as possible.

## Parties to the Case

> Canon 1476. Anyone whether baptized or not may be parties in a case. The party who is legitimately cited must respond.

The party who applies for a marital annulment is called the petitioner; the other party is called the respondent, or defendant.

## Proxies and Advocates

> Canon 1483. The proxy and advocate must be at least 18 and of good reputation. Furthermore, the advocate must be Catholic, unless the diocesan bishop permits otherwise. He/she must be a doctor in canon law, or otherwise truly expert in it; and he/she must be approved by the diocesan bishop.

A proxy is one who may represent a party in court. The advocate is the attorney for the party. In marriage cases the advocate is usually the one who presents arguments in favor of the petitioner who is seeking marital annulment.

*Witnesses*

> Canon 1549. All persons may be witnesses unless they are expressly excluded by law, either totally or partially.
> Canon 1550,1. Minors under 14 and those who are feebleminded may not be admitted as witnesses. However, they may be heard if the judge by decree declares that it is expedient.
> 2. They are incapable of serving as witnesses who are:
>> 1) the parties in the case, or those who represent the parties in the trial; the judge or his/her assistants; the advocate and others who are assisting or have assisted the parties in the same case;
>> 2) priests regarding anything which they learned from sacramental confession, even if the penitent requests a disclosure of those things; indeed, anything heard by anyone and in any manner on the occasion of confession may not be accepted as testimony.

The testimony of witnesses is often the most helpful form of proof in marriage annulment cases.

## The Process of Presumed Death of a Spouse

> Canon 1707,1. Whenever the death of a spouse cannot be proven by an authentic ecclesiastical or civil document, the other spouse is not considered free from the marriage bond unless the diocesan bishop renders a declaration of presumed death.

The absence of a spouse even for a long time is not sufficient evidence. The bishop must make an investigation based on the testimony of witnesses, the consideration of the spouse's reputation, and other indications (c. 1707,2).

## Administrative Recourse

> Canon 1733,1. It is very desirable that, whenever a
> person believes that he/she has been harmed by a
> decree, that person should avoid contention with the
> author of the decree and try to reach an equitable
> solution by mutual consultation. Other respected
> persons might also be used for mediation and study
> so that by suitable means controversy may be avoid-
> ed or resolved.

This canon refers to a potential conflict situation or dispute
between a Church administrative official and another person
who feels harmed by that official's decree. For example, if a
pastor fires a parochial school teacher on moral grounds because she has conceived a child outside a valid marriage, that
firing is an administrative act or "decree" which the teacher
might believe is harmful or unjust. In such a case the Church
recommends that the disputants settle their disagreement
among themselves or with the help of mutually acceptable persons. If this is not possible, the Code provides two principal
avenues for recourse against administrative decisions, namely,
diocesan "mediation boards" and hierarchic recourse.

## Diocesan Mediation Boards

> Canon 1733,2. The episcopal conference may deter-
> mine that in each diocese there be established on a
> permanent basis a certain office or council whose
> task, in accord with the norms established by the
> episcopal conference, is to seek and offer equitable
> solutions. If the conference does not order the estab-
> lishment of such an office or council, the bishop may
> create one on his own.

*Hierarchic Recourse*

> Canon 1737,1. The one who contends that he/she
> has been harmed by a decree may have recourse for
> any just reason to the hierarchic superior of the one
> who made the decree. Recourse can be proposed be-
> fore the author of the decree himself, who must im-
> mediately make it known to the competent hier-
> archical superior.

Recourse is an administrative "appeal." In the example under c. 1733,1 above of the pastor firing the teacher, the teacher
may make recourse directly to the bishop who is the hierarchic
superior of the pastor, or if she presents her recourse to the
pastor himself, he must send it on to the bishop. If the teacher
in turn wishes to take recourse against the bishop's judgment,
she has the possibility of a second recourse to the Apostolic See,
the hierarchic superior of the bishop. The procedures for recourse against administrative decrees are stated in cc.
1732–1739.

# Index